Audrey Gordon and **Dennis Klass** met in 1968 at the University of Chicago Hospitals, where they both worked with dying patients and their families. Both have taught courses for health care professionals, teachers, college students, and children and have published articles on death and dying in scholarly religious, and education journals and books. Gordon is an instructor at Oakton Community College near Chicago, and Klass is an associate professor at Webster College in St. Louis.

Audrey K. Gordon
Dennis Klass

THEY
NEED TO KNOW

How to Teach
Children about Death

A SPECTRUM BOOK

Prentice-Hall, Inc., Englewood Cliffs, New Jersey 07632

Library of Congress Cataloging in Publication Data

GORDON, AUDREY K
    They need to know.

    (A Spectrum Book)
    Includes bibliographies and index.
    1. Children and death. 2. Death—Psychological
aspects. 3. Death—Study and teaching. I. Klass,
Dennis, joint author. II. Title.
BF723.D3G6   155.9'37   79-161
ISBN 0-13-917104-5
ISBN 0-13-917096-0 pbk.

Editorial/production supervision by Betty Neville
Manufacturing buyer: Cathie Lenard

Printed in the United States of America

10 9 8 7 6 5 4 3 2 1

PRENTICE-HALL INTERNATIONAL, INC., *London*
PRENTICE-HALL OF AUSTRALIA PTY. LIMITED, *Sydney*
PRENTICE-HALL OF CANADA, LTD., *Toronto*
PRENTICE-HALL OF INDIA PRIVATE LIMITED, *New Delhi*
PRENTICE-HALL OF JAPAN, INC., *Tokyo*
PRENTICE-HALL OF SOUTHEAST ASIA PTE. LTD., *Singapore*
WHITEHALL BOOKS LIMITED, *Wellington, New Zealand*

To our children—
Holly, Dale, Brad, and Beth
Benjamin and Gregory—
From whom we have learned much about life

. . . healthy children will not fear life if their elders have integrity enough not to fear death.

ERIK H. ERIKSON
Childhood and Society

Contents

vii

Part II Teaching about Death

This book is about helping children to prepare for the reality of death. Parents and teachers are asking for information and guidance in teaching the children in their care about death. Some of the chapters focus primarily on education in the school setting, where we address practical matters that concern teachers and other school personnel. This book as a whole, however, is for everyone who is involved with children and adolescents.

Death education is concerned with the facts, skills, and attitudes we need to deal adequately with the meaning of death and with death fears. Society is in the midst of a change in the way it understands death. Major technological advances in medicine have caused revisions in the criteria for death and

Preface

prolongation of the dying process, which in turn have raised serious socioethical questions never asked before. We must learn anew what death is before we can teach our children how to cope with it. Death education, therefore, is something we must acquire for ourselves in order to pass it on to those who look to us to equip them for the tasks of life and death.

The book is divided into two parts. Part I, "The Child's Experience of Death," is designed to help adults to prepare themselves for their encounters with children. This includes understanding death in the modern world—especially as that world is experienced by the child—and helping the child to cope with death-related events in his or her life.

Part II, "Teaching about Death," is a structured approach to death education. Death education begins with adults' awareness of their own feelings about death, and we suggest ways to achieve this awareness. Possible goals for death education that a teacher might want to pursue in the classroom and the means to evaluate the achievement of these goals are also included. In Chapter 7 "Suggested Curricula by Grade and Goal," we hope to stimulate the teacher with ideas, methods, and resources for use in class that will augment teaching about death-related issues. Since many adults are not familiar with consumer issues related to death and dying, we have provided a basic consumer orientation to medical and funeral services that can be passed on to children. We conclude with some practical thoughts on politics within the school system and community as they might affect death education. The appendix consists of important documents that are basic to the study of death and dying, and the glossary defines the vocabulary associated with thanatological study.

We are grateful to the late Dr. Carl Nighswonger and to Dr. Elisabeth Kübler–Ross for the opportunity to share with them their work with the dying at the University of Chicago Hospitals and Clinics. Many of the ideas in this book have been tested by student teachers in our college classes, who then applied them to their own classrooms. We appreciate the feedback and criticisms we received from them, especially Paula Symes.

It takes time apart from regular duties and the support of one's colleges' administrative services to write a book. Webster College provided that time for Dennis Klass by granting him a faculty development leave during which some of this work was done. Both Oakton Community College and Webster College were very supportive throughout the life of this project.

The real drudgery—typing the manuscript—was performed ably by Vera Huber, Sunya Smith, Rose Frederick, Joni Jay, and Jeanne Sanschagrin. Our consultants gave freely of their time and advice, and though we remain responsible for what we have done with their words of wisdom, we wish to thank physician Monte Levinson, psychologist Marlene Andalman, funeral director Seymour Mandel, and librarians Ann Moedritzer and Mahalia Cox. Without the encouragement of our editor, Lynne Lumsden, none of this would have been possible.

Our collaboration has been much like a happy marriage, with its share of joys and frustrations. Our respective spouses, Mark and Carol, have good-naturedly tolerated our absences and have been gracious whenever we worked in each other's homes. For their understanding, we are truly grateful.

THE CHILD'S EXPERIENCE OF DEATH

Part **I**

In 1965 Geoffery Gorer, an English anthropologist, suggested that death had replaced sex as the unspeakable subject in the West. He said that death had become the new pornography, spoken of only in hushed tones with nervous laughter and, above all, never in the presence of children. Yet here we are writing a book about death education, trying to help people speak about death very much in the presence of children, and it does not feel like we are writing pornography. Gorer's essay was about changes that he saw taking place in British society. Sex was becoming less taboo, and death as a topic was becoming more taboo. "Our great-grandparents," Gorer wrote, "were

Death and the Child in Historical Perspective

Chapter **1**

told that babies were found under gooseberry bushes or cabbages; our children are likely to be told that those who have passed on . . . are changed into flowers or lie at rest in lovely gardens." Gorer's analysis of the past may have some truth to it, but his prophecy has proven false; for death has become an open topic of discussion in our culture, and the death education movement is rapidly including children in that discussion.

There is a kind of romanticism in our common view of history. We tend to speak of death in ages past as a natural part of the child's world in a way that makes that past look good to us. We hear about how death was an event that occurred at home with the family gathered about the bedside to hear the last words. Or we carry an image in our heads of the small family standing around a grave beside a covered wagon as they spend a moment of grief before getting on with the business of civilizing the land. We believe that our great-grandparents knew how to die and grieve gracefully and that because they could, death was not such a bad thing for them.

If we had to live in our great-grandparents' world, we probably would not keep our rose-colored view of it. Before 1900, a significant number of babies born could be expected to die before adulthood. Common childhood illnesses like whooping cough, diphtheria, and scarlet fever were the physical gauntlets all had to pass through to survive. Allergies to pollen or dust caused congestion, which brought permanent damage to lungs and made some people "sickly." Fatal accidents were common, and infections simply had to be allowed to run their course, as antibiotics did not exist. Unsanitary conditions led to ringworm, lice, and intestinal parasites, which lowered everyone's energy levels. Dying was visible, and it wasn't romantic but often ugly, harsh, and all too painful. The dead decomposed physically, assaulting the senses, and rapid burial was imperative.

Death was a frequent occurrence, the natural resolution of the apparent fragility of the human condition. Ideas about death were much more often a subject for meditation then. Old diaries and letters that speak of the writer's being in bed with a cold and thinking about the possibility of death do not show an excessive morbidity but rather reflect logical thinking about the world as it was. Since then, as public health measures have improved the physical well-being of people in such developed nations as the United States, our relationship with death has undergone dramatic changes. We cannot hope to move back to a simpler time, for both the nature of death and the relationship children have with it have changed drastically.

The world in which modern children experience death is different from any child's world of the past. Two trends over the course of this century have influenced and continue to influence the relationship between the child and death. The first is the increasing distance of the immediate experience of death from everyday life. The second is the increasing distance of the child from the adult world. Taken together, these trends have radically changed how a child can respond to death.

DEATH AS A STRANGER

We can see the increasing distance of death from everyday life by looking for a moment at some statistics. It is a statistical lie to say that the life span has increased.

What is happening is that fewer people are dying at younger ages and that more people are living toward their full life span of approximately 100 years. The advance of the *average* age of death from the forties in the 1900s to nearly eighty in the 1970s is due to the discovery and use of vaccines to prevent childhood diseases and the improvement in public health controls (of water supplies, epidemics, and so on). By cutting down on the number of very young people dying, the average life expectancy is raised considerably; after all, if one person dies at six months of age and another at seventy, the statistical life expectancy of the two is thirty-five. In 1900, the death rate for two-year-olds was about the same as it was for sixty-eight-year-olds. That is, about 80 of every 1,000 persons could be expected to die at those respective ages—approximately the death rate expected in seventy-four-year-olds today. In past generations, those who had reasonably good nutrition and limited occupational hazards lived as long as people today can expect to live—once they had survived childhood. George Washington died at sixty-seven, John Adams at ninety, Abigail Adams at eighty-four, Thomas Jefferson at eighty-three, James Madison at eighty-five, Dolley Madison at eighty-one, James Monroe at seventy-three, John Quincy Adams at eighty, and Betsy Ross at eighty-four. An overwhelming majority of people in this country now die after the age of sixty-five, and relatively few are under twenty. Death has changed from being an expected part of the child's world to a rather uncommon event. It is very possible for a child today to graduate from high school, never having experienced a significant death, since grandparents typically die when their grandchildren are between twenty and thirty.

We have encountered adolescents and adults who have never been to a funeral, because no one they knew well had thus far died.

The fact that neither the child nor the child's parents are in imminent danger of dying changes death realistically from being a self-related event to an other-related event. In his book, *Western Attitudes Toward Death,* Philippe Aries says that the whole movement in Western history has been away from understanding death as something that happens to us to thinking and feeling about death as something that happens to others. Eighteenth-century revival preachers could plunge their congregations into deep anxiety by dwelling on the ephemeral nature of human existence. Each time one of his children was sick, Cotton Mather thought and wrote about death, because he feared the child would die. Abraham Lincoln's lifelong melancholia may have originated with his mother's death when he was a child and deepened after the death of his son. But in the modern world, infections and illnesses that could formerly have brought on the possibility of death or at least of several months of recovery now cause a few days' absence from school and are seldom the occasion for pondering the fleeting nature of life by either the parent or the child. Children and parents still do die, but when it happens, it is seen as an intrusion on normal reality. It is seen as an accident or the invasion of the body by foreign microbes rather than as part of the normal human condition. Although children are very aware of death and seem to have thoughts about it as part of their normal psychological development, in their everyday lives, death has become something that happens only rarely and to somebody else. Indeed it has been observed that parental death is rare enough to have caused the virtual disappearance of the word *orphan* in the last fifty years.

FROM ECONOMICS TO EMOTION

Some scholars have wondered if the change in the death rate of children has had an effect on the web of emotional ties within the family. David Stannard (1974) notes that colonial mothers were warned to keep at a distance from their children emotionally, in part because they would be less hurt if and when the children died. Perhaps it is partly because they are less in danger of dying that the emotional ties surrounding the modern child are stronger than those in early days. Besides the change in the experience of death itself, emotional ties became more important in the modern world as the economic bonds that once held families together weakened. Families were once important units in the production of goods and services. Children were part of this economic production from their very early years and except in the highest social classes, were fully integrated into economic life by the time they reached puberty. Now, except as a consuming unit of society, the modern family has no economic function. Marriage was, until a short time ago, primarily an economic matter— either as a way to exchange property between families or as a partnership necessary to running a farm or business. Marrying for love is a recent innovation. Children began to be kept at home only a few hundred years ago. Before that, they were sent out to wet nurses as infants and apprenticed to a trade in early puberty. The traditional household included children from other families, servants, hired hands, and an assortment of husbandless women and old people. The modern child is raised by the biological parents with little outside contact until nursery school and remains a part of the nuclear family until college or marriage.

Death, then, is uncommon in the modern family's experience and so is loaded with more significance than more conventional occurrences. This more significant experience takes place in a far stronger and more complex web of emotional connections. Within the context of the nuclear family, death has changed. Once the death of the father could spell economic disaster for the family. Now, however, economic considerations play a less important role in family life. Insurance, social security, retirement benefits, and the like provide the most basic necessities for many families when the breadwinner dies. It costs a lot of money now to be sick and die, but that is consumer-oriented economics and not productive economics. When death occurs now, it is primarily a destroyer of emotional bonds. The reality of death becomes personally more threatening, whereas when death affected economic relationships, it was the consequences of death that were most troublesome. In teaching death education today, we find that we put far more emphasis on the emotional aspects of the experience, even though relatively few of our students have lived through an emotionally significant death. We do find, however, that those students who have experienced a significant death are more affected emotionally than in any other way. Although there are instances of students being compelled to drop out of school after the death of a parent so they can support the family, such hardship is increasingly less common. What we have instead are students who understand death as the end of a complex set of emotional ties from which they may not yet have developmentally separated. Since the child is apt to be less affected by the economic consequences of the death, his everyday routine changes little. Indeed, life may not seem much different except for the loss of whatever emotional attachment they had with the dead. But those emotional attachments are singularly important, for in the context of a modern understanding of development, they are the child's most important way of achieving identity and selfhood.

Since younger children may not have mastered the emotional ties within the family and since teenage children often have ambivalent feelings about those ties, it is not unusual for young people to make little overt response to a significant death. Since death has few external consequences, their lives really do not change much, and they do not know how to respond to the emotional loss. This is very normal, but we find that many children later feel guilty for not feeling what their parents or other adults expected them to feel or for not feeling what they now believe they ought to have felt. The double change death has for the modern world—physically more distant but emotionally closer—may be very confusing for some young people.

In this emotionally based modern family pattern, values are held that exclude the reality of death for children. Childhood is valued as a time of innocence and naiveté that should be prolonged as much as possible before the problems of the adult world are faced. The child represents hope in the goodness of the future. So children are protected from the harsh realities of economics and discord. Indeed, the point of a great deal of current psychotherapy is to restore to adults the self that is the "natural child." The fear-filled world of Huckleberry Finn, the threatening stories of the Brothers Grimm do not seem "right" to many modern parents. The fate of the "Three Little Pigs" is changed from two of them being eaten by the wolf to all three escaping and singing, "Who's afraid of the big bad wolf, not me!" Adults, then, may understand death, but children are protected from it, for the belief in the innocence and naiveté of childhood holds that only happy thoughts are appropriate for children. In the "Sesame Street" version of "Little Miss Muffet," the spider doesn't frighten her away; she frightens the spider.

Adults feel as though they can build a world in which the child is protected. As they face traumatic problems, they feel they should be stoic and not show their vulnerability to their children. Children are rarely asked to master the real world of mechanical objects but go instead to parks and master the romanticized skills of cliff climbing and fire-building. Rather than allowing children to find their way around a real and dangerous city, we let them find their way through a preplanned nature trail in the woods. We encourage children toward mastery in their imagination—toy race cars that really switch lanes or toy helicopters that pick up the drowning pilot—but leave the nonimaginal world to the grown-ups. If anything does go wrong in the child's world, we adults feel guilty or powerless when we cannot make it better. Since we cannot make death better, we try to protect the child from it.

DEATH'S
SPECIAL PLACES

If death has become more distant from everyday life due to its relative infrequency, the trend has also been to make it physically more distant. Two institutions have expanded their functions enormously since the turn of the century—the hospital and the funeral home. In urban areas, where the majority of people now live, nearly four of every five deaths occur away from the home—in hospitals or other institutional settings. Death takes place in institutions, because death—like many other things—has become a matter of technological manipulation. That is, death has moved from being completely out of human control to being within human control to some extent. To be sure, everyone dies; but many illnesses respond to treatment, and in those that are fatal, treatment of symptoms can delay death for some time. For example, when it is not curable, cancer can often run a course of several years with radiation, surgery, and chemotherapy, bringing cycles of hope and despair and side effects of the treatment often nearly as bad as the disease itself. When the end nears, simple measures like respiration therapy or antibiotics can delay the actual death for several weeks more. Most people do not understand modern medical procedures, so death becomes the province of experts rather than a matter that can be handled by family and friends. The setting of death is sterile, efficient, and professional. In a culture that has adopted the casual look as normative and first-name democracy in most places of work, the place of dying is formalized with uniforms and an authoritarian hierarchy surpassed only by the military.

The dying are fitted into the institutional system, surrounded mainly by people for whom caring is a profession they leave after eight hours and to whom death means the replacement of one patient by another. The death scene itself would have been science fiction only a generation ago. Machines, not people, are the predominant feature of the death room. Once a person's last words were important, but today they can rarely be uttered; for if the respirator is not blocking the vocal cords, drugs to ease the pain have put the person into a comatose state. This is the environment where family becomes "visitors" and children are excluded.

The funeral chapel did not exist as a business establishment before the Civil War. There were cabinetmakers who built coffins, livery stables that rented hearses, and drapery companies that furnished crepe. The funeral, like death itself, was essentially a home affair. The mortuary represents an interesting compromise. Americans do not want death too close to home, but they do not want the setting to seem impersonal, either. The corpse used to be laid out in the living room (once called the parlor, hence the term *funeral parlor*). So the mortuary becomes a funeral "home"—a home away from home—a reception area for public display of family and corpse, where the family can go to do their sitting and talking and then return to their real home where there are no signs of death. Children are allowed in the funeral home; however, many parents feel it is not quite right for them to be there. Unless they have visited the funeral home before, the strangeness of the place and the formality of the adults in an emotionally tense situation make it unlikely that children will be able to deal with the reality of death. The cosmeticized body and the appearance of slumber suggested by the embalmer's art also makes it unlikely—given the childhood belief in the reversibility of death—that children will be able to grasp death's finality.

It is easy to blame the medical profession or the funeral industry for the increasing distance death has for our day. But it is we who choose to use hospitals and institutions as dying places and we who choose to buy the full range of funeral services. It is not uncommon for terminally ill people who have been told that nothing more can be done for them medically to check into the hospital for their last few days or weeks, after being urged to do so by anxious families. Those of us who profess to stand firmly for simpler and more home-centered funeral customs, when confronted with an actual death, find ourselves having the deceased embalmed and displayed in an expensive casket because of family pressure or a sense of guilt. It is clear that no one forces us to hold death at such a distance. We choose the distance for ourselves for a variety of reasons that seem legitimate to us at the time. But whatever the immediate reasons, the result is that death is physically isolated from the child in modern America.

THE EMERGENCE
OF CHILDHOOD

Just as death has become more distant from the child's world, so the child has become more distant from the adult world. Philippe Aries (1962) has pointed out that the concept of the child as defined by the boundaries of biological age and development is a relatively new concept in

Western history. Until 300 years ago, the category of "child" included all people who were dependent on others in some way. Some were what we call children, but others were servants, vassals, or women. In the peasant classes, when a child could walk and talk, there was little that he or she did that distinguished the child from the elders. All played the same games, believed the same myths, attended the same festivals, and were subject to the same community sanctions. The child in past centuries did not understand or experience death in an essentially different way from adults.

If we extend Aries's thesis, we see that there was a gradual emergence of the role of children as they became a special group in the consciousness of the West. This new group was subject to sanctions and restrictions that the rest of the culture was not. It was common hundreds of years ago to include children in sexual discussions and even to include them in sex play. When children became a special group, sex became taboo for them. Gorer's (1965) article on the pornography of death in our time shows how children became sheltered by the adult community from discussion about death at the very time the earlier sheltering about sexual matters was being lifted. The reason that the taboo on discussing death may now be lifted is that children are segregated enough for the culture safely to drop some of its social barriers. There are special laws to protect children, special physicians to care for them, special teachers trained to specified age needs, and even special sex education and death education.

When we begin to think about the relationship of children and parents in terms of their interaction with death, it is possible to interpret Aries's data somewhat differently than he does. Perhaps what was really happening was not a development of the concept of child at all but the movement of the adult population away from more primitive ways of thought and toward the development of new behavior, leaving the child behind where everyone else had been before. Although this new adult consciousness may have been developing within an elite intelligentsia for some time, it is only in this century that many adults really stopped believing the things they continue to tell their children about death. Gorer notes that in the England of the 1960s, many parents were very conscious that what they told their children when someone died was not what they themselves believed. Sylvia Anthony (1972) notes similar discontinuity between what parents think and what children are told. In Anthony's study, first published in 1940, children were told different things than the children of Gorer's study. Perhaps it is because parents found they did not know what to believe and feared sharing their confusion with their children, telling the children instead what they wanted to but no longer could believe. This has a snowball effect. The children Anthony studied in her pioneering work of 1940 are themselves parents and grandparents now. Clearly these people do not now believe what they were told as children—that the dead are on a long trip, or gone to sleep, or in the sky. Recent times have seen the increasing secularization of culture, a change in traditional religious structures, and an almost dogmatic reliance upon scientific explanations to explain the nature and purpose of life. Today's parents may have had no satisfactory childhood models to handle questions about death because of rapid cultural change and so had no models to pass on to their children. In an effort to protect the child from their own doubts and confusion, parents give what they perceive to be basic scientific answers, thereby further distancing the reality of death, as the adult encounters it, from the child.

LOOKING FORWARD

Thinking about death education in this historical perspective can help us in two ways. First, it can help us to understand what can happen when we introduce honest talk with children about death and introduce death as a formal subject in the classroom. Second, it can help us to understand the modern response to death, both ours and our children's. The two long-term trends—the increasing isolation of the experience of death from everyday life and the increasing distance of the child from the adult world—form the context of our thinking about death—for ourselves and our children—and about what we as educators and parents are doing when we attempt to talk openly to our children about death.

Death education will not return us to a simpler time in our culture's death system, for we cannot—indeed we do not want to—roll back the progress of modern medical science. So death in the future will remain a technologically controlled event. Further scientific breakthroughs may increase the level of technological manipulation surrounding death. People will continue to die toward the end of the life span and may continue to be treated primarily in institutions, though being at home for the actual death may increase. For this reason, it is unrealistic to expect that death education will greatly diminish the distance between the modern child and death. But increasingly, the decisions about medical treatment and the artificial prolongation of life are shared by physicians, patients, and family. Among the goals we recommend for death education are the clarification of values on which to base life-and-death decisions and the securing of information to help make those decisions. If older children can participate in discussions leading to decisions about life and death, they will be closer to the death process and to the questions of the meaning of life itself.

It is possible that the function of the funeral home will change in our children's lifetime. Changes that seem to be taking place are in the direction of faster body disposal and less public recognition of the death with less communal mourning. This increases the distance between the child and death. If death education fosters an increased public recognition of death and facilitates more community-oriented and holistic mourning patterns, it may serve to decrease this distance.

The family will probably remain an emotionally based unit, and children will continue to enjoy a special conflict-free and economically dependent role in the family; but if death education is successful, the gap between the child's world and the adult's world in understanding death will narrow. Parents and children can share the same facts about death and can be in communication about the significance death has for the parents' life philosophy and for the child's emerging meaning system. If, however, the distance between the child's world and our own is to be closed, those values will change that hold childhood to be a time of innocence when adults shelter children from the harsh realities of life, at least in respect to death. We cannot communicate openly with our children about death and still protect them from it. This means a change in the way death has been handled in the culture as a whole, for to communicate freely about it and to face up to the values and decisions that death presents us is to accept death in a way Americans have been unwilling to do up to now.

Let's look ahead to see how death education could possibly influence the future development of the relationship between children and death. Widespread teaching about death will probably change the historical context within which the next generation works. If, for example, over the next fifteen years, we see a trend away from dying in institutions toward dying at home, we might postulate a correlation between that trend and death education, thereby claiming that death education functioned to decrease the distance of death from everyday life. So, too, if the explanations of death that children are given in school are accepted as valid by parents, education will have functioned directly to decrease the distance between the child and the adult world. If the funeral industry changes to meet new consumer demands for simpler services, we might be able to attribute that change to death education as well.

The question is what happens after a taboo has been lifted; to use Gorer's language—what happens when that which has been pornographic becomes "clean." The question is not an abstract one, for taking the taboo away from death is a change that is happening in our culture now, and death education is a major part of the change. It is very dangerous, of course, to analyze the effects of ideas that are still in flux. Things are so much clearer after a few generations. But now is when we have to make decisions and find meaning, so analysis is necessary.

There is ample statistical and anecdotal evidence that Gorer's thesis about death as a taboo subject is right. In one survey, almost 98 percent of the respondents said they had not discussed the topic of death with friends recently, yet there is an abundance of lecturing and writing about death. Elisabeth Kübler–Ross's books on death have been best-sellers. People are beginning to talk and read about death, and that discussion and literature are making their way into the school. So what happens when that which has been pornographic emerges into the open?

We might look at death education's older sibling, sex education, for some insight. Three things can be noted that happened in the culture as sex became less taboo. First, nontabooed sexuality became part of and indeed contributed to a larger movement of self-centered, individualistic hedonism. Whereas such early exponents of sex education as Wilhelm Reich wanted the breaking of sexual repressions in order to experience the development of community, what seems to be happening now is that freed sexuality becomes a way of narcissistically gratifying the self, thereby atomizing community. We might ask the question: "Does focusing attention on individual death and making individual death more meaningful only enable us to turn our back on a larger world that faces impending universal death from nuclear warfare and ecological destruction?" Or, phrased differently, "Does death education help to further privatize death instead of returning it to communal interaction?" These are sociological developments that have important consequences for our moral and psychological survival.

Second, sex has not so far been made a holistic part of our understanding but has retained its separateness from its taboo days. The current proliferation of sex therapies is geared to sexual practice that is isolated from other aspects of human life such as economics and religion. Sexual development is often understood by itself, as another standard by which people judge themselves, and that standard is not connected to understanding the person in a total way.

Third, the greatest interest in sex after lifting the taboo seems to be on technique and not on meaning. Many people who have read Kübler–Ross's books use her five stages of dying essentially as technique, going through the process with their finger in the book for easy reference when they do not know what to do next. Robert Kastenbaum has wondered with some irony if the "climax" of the current change in attitudes toward death will be a book called *The Joy of Dying*, complete with instructions on all the various possibilities together with realistic illustrations. The same possibilities exist in the lifting of the taboo from death information as existed in the lifting of the taboo from sex information. Death education might have some unforeseeable and unwelcome components. Students might become calloused or glib about death. Comfort with the idea of death could make suicide more romantic or less frightening at certain vulnerable ages in adolescent development. The more philosophic and religious views of death may give way to sheer pragmatism, which will rob us of the opportunity to see death as a stimulus for creative belief, courage, and hope for the future. We can be alert to these possible pitfalls.

But if understanding death and dying and the grieving process will help to prevent the emotional scarring and permanent damage that a significant death can cause a family, then we will have accomplished a great deal. If death education can make us wiser consumers of medical and funeral services, then we can improve the services these professions offer. And if death education can help us to define the quality of life and the dignity of the individual in a community of other individuals, then how can society lose? If death education helps everyone to confront the idea that we will all die, then perhaps the meaning we find in death will transcend the individual and help us to become part of a community of shared belief and commitment. What we do in school and at home with our children may help to change the world; and if what we do reflects emerging social values, then as we plan our units at school and discuss death with our students and children, we need to set our goals within the larger framework and goals of society.

FURTHER READING

ANTHONY, SYLVIA, *The Discovery of Death in Childhood and After*. New York: Basic Books, 1972.

ARIES, PHILIPPE, *Centuries of Childhood*, Robert Baldick, trans. New York: Vintage Books, 1962.

————, *Western Attitudes Toward Death*. Baltimore, Md.: Johns Hopkins University Press, 1974.

COMPER, FRANCES, M. M., trans., *The Book of the Craft of Dying and Other English Tracts Concerning Death*. New York: Green & Co., 1917.

DEMAUSE, LLOYD, ed., *The History of Childhood*. New York: Harper & Row, 1974.

GORER, GEOFFREY, *Death, Grief, and Mourning*. Garden City, N.Y.: Doubleday, 1965.

GREEN, B. R., AND D. P. IRISH, eds., *Death Education: Preparation for Living*. Cambridge, Mass.: Schenkman Publishing Co., 1971.

JACKSON, CHARLES, *Passing: The Vision of Death in America*. Westport, Conn.: Greenwood Press, 1977.

SHORTER, EDWARD, *The Making of the Modern Family*. New York: Basic Books, 1975.

STANNARD, DAVID, ed., *Death in America*. Philadelphia, Pa.: University of Pennsylvania Press, 1974.

On the day Socrates was to drink the hemlock and die, he and his disciples talked about the meaning of death. As they debated, trying to prove that death was a good thing, especially for philosophers, they kept running into blank walls as argument after argument failed. Socrates said to the discouraged disciples, "Like children, you are haunted with a fear that when the soul leaves the body, the wind may really blow her away and scatter her." Cebes, one of the disciples, gave a smile of recognition and said, "Strictly speaking, they are not our fears, but there is a child within us to whom death is a sort of hobgoblin; him too we must persuade not to be afraid when he is alone

Children and Their Responses to Death

Chapter **2**

with him in the dark." The discussion that day, as reported in *Phaedo*, was only partly successful, and many of
them ended the day as sadly as they had begun it. For
indeed, the fearful child within them would not be calmed
in the face of this important death in their life.

This chapter is a brief survey of the research on children's developmental ideas of death and their observed
emotional response. As we try to understand children and
their response to death, we find that we are not really different from the Athenian disciples, for when we try to understand children, we recognize the child within us, especially when we are alone in the dark. When the veneer
of our adulthood is stripped away in our dreams or when
we are under stress, our own emotions surface, and we
recognize the children we once were beneath the adults
we have become. As adults, we have learned to give reasonable and scientific answers to questions like "Why did
he die?" and the more difficult "Why must I die?" That is,
we have learned to separate the world into different com-
partments of reason, emotion, and belief. Young children
have not yet learned to make such separations. Very often
the smiles we have for the child's ideas are smiles of
recognition—a connection we can make with our own experience. So we really understand the child. But our smile
may also be the use of humor to ward off an uncomfortable answer because it is too close to what we fear may be
true. We laugh to assure ourselves that their answer is not
true. Yet the adult explanations fall apart when the facade
of the rational self is pulled away by crisis or pain. There
are few people, for example, who—when they learn they
may very well die—do not for long moments consider that
death is a punishment for some real or imagined wrong.
There are some grieving adults who believe angry wishes

expressed in words like "drop dead," whether said or unsaid, caused the death. One of our children once hypothesized that everyone was given a certain amount of numbers. First you are one, then you are two, three, and so on. When you run out of numbers, you die. The child shows the objectifying of numbers characteristic of a three-year-old, but is such a theory really so different from the adult shrug, "When your number is up. . . ."?

IDEAS ABOUT DEATH

The children with whom we interact are going through the process of developing conceptual models for understanding death. They are people with special ways of seeing the world at this time in their lives, but there is no single mold into which all children fit. There is as much diversity in young people's ideas about death as there is diversity in their ideas about anything else. There seem to be no innate ideas that children inevitably have about death; that is, there are almost as many answers by children at a given age about death as it is possible to give. Some people have noted that the child's answers are similar to the answers nontechnological, traditional people (they used to be called primitive people) gave when questioned by anthropologists. Researchers concluded that the child's concept of death was developmental, following the same pattern as the evolutionary development of the species—Ontogeny recapitulates phylogeny—can apply even to concepts of death.

Sylvia Anthony (1972), a pioneer in the study of children and death, has refuted such ideas. She says that children and nontechnological peoples draw *logical* conclusions from what they can observe in the world:

1. They see that the body is perceived as separate from the soul, for when we sleep at night, we see and feel things that clearly do not require our bodily participation.
2. When infants learn object constancy, they understand that objects in their environment are separate from themselves.
3. Time goes only one way for everyone.
4. Everything a child can identify as living also dies. Even those children who identify life with movement—clouds and the sun's daily path, for example—know that the clouds disappear and the sun goes away.

Another factor influencing children in the formation of their ideas is that the language they are learning to use has many strange references to death. The car will not start because the battery is dead. In a dart game, while "killing" time, someone once threw one "dead" center. An exasperated father yells to "kill" the light after he has come home "dead" tired, because he has spent all day with "deadbeats" who are trying to make a "killing in the market." On the other hand, adult language tries to avoid the use of the words *dead* or *die* when death itself is actually spoken about. So we put pets "to sleep," and people "pass on" or are "lost" or "expire" when we really mean they are dead. No wonder children have trouble understanding what we're saying to them!

Putting all the things they see together with the language they hear and making no effort to separate "what" from "why," prekindergarten children often supply very creative theories about death and dying. One of the most common is that death and birth are cycles within the same entity. Anthony found that many children thought that putting a dead body in water would bring it back to life. Others theorized that the cycle was within a larger cosmic system, so that in order for one person to be born, it was necessary that someone else die.

In an effort to find out just how children (ages five to fourteen) develop in their ability to understand death, Anthony inserted the word *dead* into a vocabulary list on the Terman–Merrill intelligence test. She then judged the answer on a scale that measured the degree to which the answer approximated an adult scientific definition rather than an emotional definition occurring in crisis situations. The degrees of knowledge with regard to an understanding of the definition of death are:

A. Apparent ignorance of the word *dead*.
B. Interest in the word or fact combined with limited or erroneous concepts.
C. No evidence of non-comprehension of the meaning of *dead*, but definition by referrence to (a) associated phenomena not biologically or logically essential, or (b) humanity specifically.
D. Correct, essential but limited reference.
E. General, logical or biological definition or description. (Adult)

Two-thirds of the children tested answered in the C category. The scale, however, does tend to be related to mental age. No child below mental age 8 answered D and E, while no child above the mental age of 8 answered A and B. No child under five years old answered C, D or E. (Anthony, 1972, p. 49)

The two-thirds of the answers given in the C category

include definitions of dead as "when you're in your coffin," and "somebody that's been killed," and "when you go to heaven if you've been good." As Anthony shows by defining the category in the negative, the children's answers clearly show that the children know what death is. They are not able to construct an abstract definition but fall back instead upon concrete instances of death within their experience or imagination. The D category has the example, "when you are dead you can't come alive again," and in the E category, death is "a body that has no life in it." These two advanced categories show no more knowledge of what death is; they only show a greater ability to abstract. If we compare children's definitions of something we are sure they have experienced, like sickness, we see similar limitation in answers based on their ability to abstract but not limitation based on knowledge of what sickness is. When children define sickness as "when you throw up" or "a time when you can't go to school," we can be sure they know what it is to be sick, but they can only express their knowledge in concrete experiential terms.

A majority of children of elementary school age give answers in the C category. The creative answers children give for levels A and B are not innately wrong ideas but are logical thoughts based on their information and experience at their level of cognition. We can say that death is a subject of intellectual inquiry and interest as early as age three. Before entrance to kindergarten, the child's answers are based on common sense, observable information, and fantasy. After age five, the child formulates answers based on the information given by the adult community (including adult fantasies and beliefs). This means that from the earliest school years, the child can be expected to understand what is being taught about death in a factual way if death is presented factually.

Studies in cognitive development by Piaget and others allow us to understand research on how children respond to death, for children understand ideas at their own cognitive level. For children at the preoperational level (two and one-half to six years), things are as they appear to be, and they will remain so. Life is the experience of movement, and they attribute life to all things that move. So the concept of human life has no special significance. On the other hand, the absence of movement can denote the quality of nonaliveness or death. When a child thinks about persons or things in nature that have died, he or she attributes to them all the qualities they had when they were alive. Thus the dead can be in a box or in the sky eating, drinking, playing, or doing whatever they remember them as characteristically doing. The child can only grasp the known world, so talk about the death of parents will be tied to feelings about the death of the child's own parents. Since the preoperational child cannot assume the place of the other, the child assumes that her or his feelings about death are the same as adult emotions, and children may try to comfort adults by sharing their ideas and feelings with them.

> Mrs. A., the nursery school teacher, found the classroom pet duck dead one morning. She brought the dead duck to the children, so they could see and talk about it, remembering how much fun they had playing with it. Some weeks later, the grandfather of one of the children died, and the mother reported to Mrs. A. that the child had comforted her by telling about the duck and saying that she would remember the good things about Grandpa just as the child now remembered the good times he had with the duck.

Since the child takes adult admonitions quite literally, explanations about causes of death may be associated with things the child has heard—warnings not to play in traffic or cross the street. Explanations may be based on fiction such as television programs where death is shown unrealistically and often associated with violence.

Children at the concrete operational level, from about five to ten, are limited to specific causes and actual or possible occurrences but are able to divorce the idea of death from that of their own death or the death of their parents. Death in this stage is understood as final but far away, and as we will see in Nagy's research, it is usually personified.

> Danny's father died when he was eight years old. A few days after the funeral, Danny told his mother that his father's soul had spoken to him from a box on the closet shelf. Danny at eight could recognize the abstract concept of the soul after death but externalized and concretized it as a voice in a shoe box. Perhaps he was also semantically confused by the words *soul* and *sole*, as the child's language use at this age is literal.

At both the preoperational and concrete operational levels, death is often associated with sleep—for example, in a six-year-old's definition of death as "you're laying down and you don't know anything" or "you go to sleep forever." The idea, of course, is reinforced by common euphemisms in our language, identifying death with a sleeplike state. The idea can become problematic when going to sleep is associated with fear of dying. Several adults have reported that the childhood prayer, "Now I lay me down to sleep . . ." was the focus of major childhood fears about death. Death is also often associated with other separations. We hear this in the expressions "you never see them again" or "you can't come back any more." The ideas of old age and death are causally related in such statements as that of the seven-year-old to his grandmother, "You are old and will die soon, but mom and dad are newer." Under emotional stress, older children and adults often regress to these earlier stages of emotional response.

The formal operational level, from about eleven on, is comparable to adult ideas about death. Fifth and sixth graders begin to express emotions and intellectual processes more like the adult (denial, anger, depression, and so on), with philosophic interest in the meaning of death. They appropriate socially given explanations essentially as they are found in the culture. They may also question social customs or rituals at death, showing that they do not accept our view of the world uncritically. An eleven-year-old said: "My grandfather was all dressed up with makeup on and shoes. We had to buy a new suit, and it's going to rot anyway. I don't know why they did that." Though the form of the thought may be concrete, it is clear from this kind of attitude that he can separate this life from whatever ideas he may have of another life. One ten-year-old in defining death thought at length and finally said: "You're at rest, and nobody can bother you. In a way it's good and not bad. I imagine my grandpa in heaven, sitting in a chair with a big cigar in his mouth and no bills to pay." Older children can separate different experiences of death according to social value and meaning. A thirteen-year-old reporting on the death of his dog said: "It's sad when you don't have any brothers and you have a dog and he dies. It's like losing a brother." Since they do not have to tie all thinking about death to their own experience, they can be rather theoretical as in the definition of death as "a way to get rid of people and get ready for new people" or simply, "the end of the life cycle." Instead of being caught in their emotional experiences of death, the formal operational level allows the child to reflect on the self such as in the statement, "I don't like the words *die*, or *dead*, or *kill*. . . ."

EMOTIONS
SURROUNDING
DEATH

There has been more work done on the child's emotional response to death than on the intellectual response, though there is not at this time a consensus among scholars as to what this response is. Psychologists often look more closely at the preschool years, so much of the research is not directly useful to teachers, counselors, and parents of school-age children. Since there is no real agreement, we present some of the most significant research findings and then try to draw some usable conclusions.

Maria Nagy's work (1948) forms a kind of transition between intellectual understanding and emotional response. She asked 378 children between three and ten years old to tell whatever came to their minds on the subject of death. Older children wrote, and some younger children drew pictures. She found three stages. In the first stage, up to five years, children do not see death as final. Rather, death is a departure or reversible like sleep and is not separated from life. They think the dead can still eat, talk, and so on; it is just that they do it under the ground, or in heaven, or even on earth sometimes. The most frightening idea that death represents for the preschooler is separation from the mothering person.

Nagy's second stage is from about age five through nine. Death is understood as final but personified as a bogeyman, skeleton, or other culturally given symbol. The personification is external, so death can be escaped by running away or hiding or by recitation of magical formulas. Many examples of Nagy's second stage occur in the popular culture, from the Grim Reaper of the Middle Ages or the headless horseman in Irving's "Legend of Sleepy Hollow" to Darth Vadar in *Star Wars*. Nagy says the third stage begins after nine years and is essentially like adult ideas about death.

There are some highly speculative theories about children and death. One of the most speculative yet thought-provoking is that infants have a fear of nonbeing that later becomes the fear of death when they are old enough to conceptualize. Adah Maurer (1966) thinks that the game peek-a-boo is a way the infant masters the innate fear of nonbeing that is brought on by breaks in the child's perception of the mother's presence, such as when the child sleeps or cries for the absent mother. She says peek-a-boo comes from an Old English phrase meaning "life or death." In playing the game, a child comes to be in charge of who is there and who is not. Maurer says that as the child grows older, the game "all gone" does the same thing.

In a psychoanalytically based study, Gregory Rochlin (1967) writes that children are born with an understanding that life has limits and that they will die but that those thoughts are just too threatening. So as a defense, the young child develops infantile narcissism—or feelings of being omnipotent and omnipresent. Rochlin says that it is out of this defense against the fear of death that the ego and later the superego develop. So for Rochlin, an instinctive defense against an innate fear of death is the basis for the entire development of personality.

Perhaps Maurer's and Rochlin's theories can tell us about ourselves as adults when confronted by death. Perhaps these theories can tell us something about the way our students respond; however, what they convey about young children before the age of three is speculative.

It is Anthony, again, who has given the most significant clues to childhood fears of death. She gave children (ages five to fourteen) open-ended stories and had them complete the stories. She found that the majority of references to death came from these story openings:

> -One Sunday the boy went out for the day with his father and mother; when they came home in the evening, the mother was very sad. Why?
>
> -One night he cried when he went to bed; he was very unhappy. Why was that?
>
> -He woke up in the middle of the night and was very frightened. Why?

She found that there were two kinds of responses to these story openings: sorrow and fear. Sorrow came from fears of separation from a parent, although in the first opening, the sorrow originates in the mother's sadness because of the death of the father. Fear occurs in the context of violent aggression. The children associated death with a violent external source, either from outside the home—like a burglar—or inside the home—like a ghost. We can see that this last finding is very much like Nagy's state in which the child personified and externalized death as an aggressive enemy.

Some studies of older children throw some light on the relationship of death thoughts and fears to other aspects of adolescents' lives. It seems that bright, emotionally mature, and healthy adolescents can deal with death and thoughts of death better than those who have problems that show up in other areas as well. In another study (1964), Maurer asked 172 high school girls to write an essay on, "What comes to your mind when you think about death?" She then grouped the essays by the number of fear words used and correlated that with the level of academic achievement. She found that poor achievers had a greater fear of death, showing separation anxiety and remnants of beliefs in ghosts (Nagy's second stage) as well as preoccupation with disease and violence. Low achievers often mentioned physical things like the smell of corpses. Chalmers and Reichen (1954) found a similar relationship between other areas and death thoughts and fears when they compared normal high school girls and institutionalized subnormal girls. The subnormal girls were more likely to be overtly afraid of death, expressing thoughts and feelings about life and death more often than the normal population.

The research on children's ideas about death and their emotional response to death is scattered and often confusing. When we look at the research as a whole, however, we can make some generalizations that might be useful. It seems clear that problems about the fear of death and thoughts about dying do not seem to exist by themselves but are connected with other problems in life. If a child is having a hard time in his or her relationship with parents, peers, or schoolwork, there is a greater chance that child will also have some problems with death. This does not mean that every child has difficulty with the idea of death, but it does mean that if one does have a problem with death, the chances are good that it will be mixed with a complex of other affective material. Death fears are closely connected to other conflicts the child experiences. The other affective material frequently relates to feelings of aggression. When children personify death as a violent external aggressor, very often it is the projection of their violent aggressive feelings against those close to them. They cannot admit to themselves their anger and violent feelings toward parents, school, or whomever, so they externalize and become fearful of the bogeyman or preoccupied with the fear of lingering and deforming illnesses. All children at some point think of death as external and personified, but it becomes problematic when that personification becomes involved in the projection of their own aggression in a way harmful to their functioning.

When the problematic material is not related to aggression by an external force, the death-related material will very likely be centered around separation, especially fear of being separated from the mothering parent, but also related to fear of abandonment ("How will I survive if no one will take care of me?"). If the child has experienced the death of a parent, the fear of abandonment feels very real. This in turn may become self-blame, feelings of unworthiness, and fear that the child's own aggression caused the loss or abandonment. Fear of separation is less likely in environments where relationships are stable and predictable, although—as some psychologists think—we all have such fears deep within our psyche. Where a child's relationships are not predictable and stable, fears of separation become central. For young children bereft of a parent through death or divorce, the environment may prove to be unstable and unpredictable through that fact alone.

If those psychologists who think there are instinctive defense mechanisms against death ("playing peek-a-boo") in the first few years are correct, the question then is, "Why isn't every schoolchild a mass of neuroses about death?" Some philosophers like Ernest Becker (1973) believe that actually we all are, or ought to be, neurotic about death. But the people who ask questions of children find that by and large, they understand what death is and don't think about it too much, and when they do think about it, they seem to be able to handle it appropriately for their ages. If there are harmful or inappropriate ways of dealing with death, it would seem that they don't appear at school age more than they do in adults, unless there have been problems like extreme family conflicts, bad school adjustment, or traumatic losses in the early years. Perhaps the current interest in death will inspire more research, but for now it would appear that the percentage of schoolchildren with problematic emotional responses to death is about the same as that in the adult population.

We have learned a good deal about children since that day Socrates talked with his disciples. In learning about children, we have learned about ourselves. The fear of separation and the externalization of aggression as a fear of violent death are not psychological dynamics for the child alone. The mixing of problematic fears of death and other problems in life is not limited to the years of childhood development. We can recognize the behavior of the child by being sensitive to our own child within and by recognizing that those feelings in us that we sometimes label as being out of control, or magical, or vulnerable come from the child within each of us.

FURTHER READING

ANTHONY, SYLVIA, *The Discovery of Death in Childhood and After*. New York: Basic Books, 1972.

BECKER, ERNEST, *Denial of Death*. New York: Free Press, 1973.

BLUEBOND-LANGNER, MYRA, *The Private Worlds of Dying Children*. Princeton, N.J.: Princeton University Press, 1978.

BOWLBY, JOHN, *Attachment and Loss*. New York: Basic Books, 1969.

CHALMERS, STACY, and MARIE REICHEN, "Attitudes Toward Death and Future Life Among Normal and Subnormal Adolescent Girls," *Exceptional Children*, 20 (1954), 259–62.

FURTH, HANS G., *Piaget for Teachers*. Englewood Cliffs, N.J.: Prentice-Hall, 1970.

HOSTLER, SHARON L., "The Development of Child's Concept of Death, in *The Child and Death*, ed. Olle Jane Sahler. St. Louis, Mo.: C. V. Mosby Co., 1978.

MAURER, ADAH, "Adolescent Attitudes Toward Death," *Journal of Genetic Psychology*, 105 (1964), 79–90.

——, "Maturation of the Concept of Death," *British Journal of Medicine and Psychology*, 39 (1966), 35–41.

NAGY, MARIA, "The Child's View of Death," *Journal of Genetic Psychology*, 73 (1948), 3–27.

PIAGET, JEAN, *The Child's Conception of the World*, Joan and Andrew Tomlinson, trans., Totowa, N.J.: Littlefield, Adams, & Co., 1967.

PIAGET, JEAN, and BARBEL INHELDER, *The Psychology of the Child*. New York: Basic Books, 1969.

ROCHLIN, GREGORY, "How Younger Children View Death and Themselves," in *Explaining Death to Children*, ed. Earl Grollman. Boston: Beacon Press, 1967.

Death confronts us and our children in many ways. There are no simple, standard rules we can call on to help young people understand and cope with death except the principle of keeping the lines of communication open within the family and the community. Different situations have within them special dangers and unique growth opportunities for us and for our children.

We have compiled a list of the questions we are most often asked by parents and teachers, combining some into questions that cover generalized situations. This chapter is organized around those questions with answers that speak broadly to each situation presented. But each per-

Helping the Child Handle Death

Chapter **3**

son and each confrontation with death is unique, and our answers can only be general outlines into which parents and teachers must put their self-understanding and their understanding of the children with whom they are interacting. The bibliography we have provided for this chapter is longer than that for the others, because we have tried to address so many different areas. Parents and teachers who want to read more about areas discussed can find books and articles in the bibliography that will help.

My child is dying. Shall I tell my child? When? And how can I cope with this?

Death has a different meaning for children than for adults. Under the age of three, children fear being separated from the nurturing parent and need reassurances of safety and parental presence. For children this young, separation and abandonment involve the same sense of loss, whether permanent or temporary. Since the young child has no concept of time, he or she also cannot conceive of death in adult terms. Illness is perceived as pain and being different from other children. As soon as children can talk, they want to know what is happening to them, if it will hurt, and whether or not someone will be there. Their illness will likely bring them into hospitals—rooms full of strange equipment and people using words they don't understand. From three to six, children have a growing awareness of the finality of death but continue to fear separation and abandonment rather than dying itself. There is a great need for physical comforting for pain and answering questions honestly about treatment in a simple fashion. If a child asks directly about his or her impending death, answer directly, honestly, and hopefully with as much love and support as can be offered at such a difficult time. It is important to answer childrens' questions at the level at which they are asked and not to overload the answer with adult interpretations and emotions. Children at this age can become very sophisticated about medical treatment, comparing drugs and doctors. They know when their hospital playmates die and may be curious about where they went, how they got there, and who can play with their toys now. They can be sad about going away but do not mirror the hysteria or depression of the parents. Rather, they talk about dying or their lack of future in an angry or resigned way. They seem to tolerate painful medical procedures better than adults. Dying children perceive what's happening to them but know that adults have difficulty talking about it, so they remain silent with adults and talk with other dying children when in the clinic or hospital setting.

Older children should be told how sick they are. Parents might want to wait with this news until the child asks or until health deteriorates significantly enough to interrupt normal activities. If the family atmosphere changes drastically because of the eventual death of the child, perhaps the child should be told that the illness is very serious and that is why everyone in the family is upset. Gradually, the child will understand the seriousness of the illness and will ask questions. There is no reason to consider withholding the fact that they are seriously ill, for all dying children have some awareness that they pick up from ever-present clues in their personal interactions with others. By pretending there is nothing wrong, we put a wall between us and our child, forcing ourselves to use our energy to remember the fictions we are telling rather than in responding to what the child is saying and need-ing. Children between seven and twelve will receive in-formation from us and the medical staff jointly. After age twelve, the child will probably get information from the medical staff in the same way an adult would. Children between seven and twelve can also communicate more directly with their doctor about their illness because of their increased ability to understand.

The morality of children during latency (ages seven to eleven) is highly developed, with an acute sense of con-science and right and wrong behavior. They have a sense of individuation and can usually understand that death is final. In addition to the earlier fears of separation or aban-donment, children of this age will feel that their death is a punishment for some real or imagined wrong. Their fan-tasies, as seen in their drawings and stories, may be of a personified death—a dark figure who is waiting to snatch them away—or of bodily mutilation or harm. The child needs a supportive environment in which those fears and guilt feelings can be expressed and rationally examined. But such an environment cannot be created when parental anxiety and guilt block honest communication of feelings. Loving communication between parents and child in-cludes the child's need to express negative emotions and fears about death and the parents' need to express sorrow.

Teenage children get their information in the same way adult patients do. By this time, the fear of separation has faded as a response to death, because the adolescent is well on the way to an identity separate from us. Although guilt may still be a response to death, the adolescent is likely to rage against the world for cutting off the pos-sibilities that had just begun. Adolescents don't talk about their anger, because they haven't been given permission to express anger freely. For adolescents, the question "Why me?" can take on great significance, because they are in the stage Erik Erikson calls identity seeking, and that involves exploring ideologies that show the structure of the physical, moral, and interpersonal world. We may have to spend long hours discussing the meaning of life and death with these older children. In terms of their relationship to ideology, if the adolescent can relate his or her death to a larger cause, death will be more understandable.

We as parents have many important tasks. We need to find constructive channels for our grief, keep communication open between the dying child and the rest of the family, and try to interpret what is happening for the dying child and for the other children in the family. We must provide a secure parental bond for the dying child at the very time that we prepare to sever our investment in the child's future. If we are to serve our child best, we need to serve ourselves by finding ways of expressing our grief that do not interfere with our relationship with the child and that do not seriously impair the family relationships that will continue after the child's death.

Grief can take many forms. No two ways of grieving are exactly the same, and we may respond in only one way; or at different stages, we may respond many different ways. If we repress much of our grief, we may think we are not responding strongly enough to the death of our child. We can be angry at the world and sometimes angry at the child who is dying; we can want to isolate ourselves and live in a protective cocoon; we can be impatient for the long ordeal to end and at times want the child to die, so we can get over our pain and start living normally again. We feel guilty because we think somehow we did something to cause the child's dying; guilt can take the form of being overly solicitous to the child and allowing him or her to make excessive demands, or we can fear our feelings of guilt and withdraw from the child. We can project our guilt on others (especially our spouse), blaming them for the impending death. Lack of awareness of these feelings can cause many problems in a previously stable marriage. Within a few years after the death of a child, many couples divorce or go through a period of emotional separation. Studies indicate that the grief they have been through has severely strained the relationship.

We need to get our support systems lined up as soon as we realize how sick the child is. Support systems are made up of those people with whom we can break down and cry; those to whom we dare express the scary and angry thoughts; those we can ask for extra child-care or physical help. It is hard enough being a parent and harder being a working parent. The mere physical demands of the child's illness impose a strain on our time and energy. We need to be at the hospital for long periods of time and still get the shopping done and the bills paid. In many families, it is one of the relatives who takes over much of the day-to-day duties so the parents can devote themselves to the dying child. In those families who do not live near relatives, some other homemaking help often must be arranged.

But we also need to provide for our emotions. Though some of us may try to keep all our feelings inside, we really do better if we can "get it off our chest" once in a while. Sometimes an understanding friend can be available for this, but often we need to find a counselor, clergyperson, social worker, or physician who can be understanding when we feel vulnerable, reasonable when we are unreasonable, and supportive when we break down.

What we have to give our dying child, then, is ourselves. This is often not an easy job, for our own grief intervenes in the process of breaking the tie between us. We must try to avoid cutting off our emotional attachment to the child before the child actually dies. Especially with children who are never taken home from the hospital or who are institutionalized within the first few months, many parents find it easier to function as if the child is already gone and turn their attention to the remaining family. It is not difficult to understand such a response to very young infants who never had a chance to share significant portions of our lives. However, the children who have become part of our lives—the children we have nursed through sleepless nights and played peek-a-boo with—are attached to us and we to them; so although it hurts, we have to be with them to the end. Ida Martinson in *Home Care for the Dying Child* tells how most children can die at home in loving surroundings. There are wise physicians and counseling services that will help us cope with the dying child at home. This can be a rewarding family experience and will not be a traumatic event for other children at home. Very young children fear separation more than death itself. Our presence and familiar surroundings are the most reassuring gifts we can give to the dying child. If the medical situation is such that the child and the family are better off emotionally with the child in the hospital setting, then this alternative must be taken instead of home care.

A dying child puts a strain on all relationships in the family. As in many other crisis situations, we can use them for growth, or the crises will weaken already strained relationships. Some families feel abandoned when a parent spends all waking hours at the hospital with an ailing child. Our feelings can take many strange twists, and we often do not realize what is going on in us until it explodes. For example, a man whose infant was in the hospital coped badly when his wife also had to be hospitalized for an infection. He found that he was angry with his sick wife, because "it is her job" to be with the sick baby. Some wives feel that a husband who is busy with practical details and money is not supporting them emotionally. Few marriages are perfect, and the imperfections are magnified by the crisis while the amount of time the couple can spend together to work through problems is radically shortened. It takes a lot of love and communication between husband and wife to weather this kind of crisis—and such love must include forgiveness. The other children will have to find their own way to come to terms with their sibling's dying. This may not be an easy process, but it can be used as a growth experience if we do our best to keep in communication with them. They may feel left out of our lives when we pull out of their lives somewhat in order to devote our energy and attention to the dying child and to our own grief. They may feel threatened by their own fears of death as they face the death of their sibling. We cannot hide reality from the other children but must include them in major family decisions and disclosures. Attempts to hide the seriousness of the family's problems will make the children mistrustful and fearful of parental actions. Older children may resent the extra chores we ask of them, but we can try to help them use the chores as a way of being more a part of the adult social system than children are usually allowed to be. If we expect more of older children, however, we may want to think about giving them more independence in other parts of their lives. They too will have to work through their feelings in their encounter with death, but grieving within the context of a compassionate and sensitive family setting helps the other children observe and experiment with models for grieving and leaves them with the confidence that they can handle troublesome emotions when they reoccur in later years. The same love and communication we need with our spouse must also be part of our relationship with our children.

The question of the relationship between the dying child and the school also is an important one. School is an integral part of the child's life, just as the adult has appointed tasks and responsibilities that must be carried out on a daily basis. If the adult is told that he or she can no longer go to work or perform necessary tasks, then that adult may feel useless, unproductive, and unwanted. If we tell the child he or she cannot go to school, the child may feel the same way and will also feel singled out and different in a negative way. When children are physically able to go to school or to be tutored at home or hospital, they should be encouraged to continue with their studies. The parents may feel, "What's the use?" but it helps the child to cope better with all the other unscheduled things in his or her life. If the child is at school, the teacher and school administration should be aware of the physical condition of the child as well as any other special problems that may arise. The school must be especially sensitive in its handling of the child so as not to make the child feel pitied or an object of constant sympathy. The teacher, as well as the parent, should be firm about holding the child to whatever academic and behavioral standards the child is truly able to meet.

Death often brings the meaningfulness of life into question, and the death of a child tests our faith and life philosophies. In helping others face death, we have found that all we really have to give is ourselves, the purpose we find in life, and the love we feel for others. That is what we have to offer to the dying child, to our spouse, and to our other children. What we get from them is the love they have to offer in return.

Should a child visit a dying relative in the hospital?

One of the difficult things about death today is that often children are kept away from the place of dying. This unnatural exclusion is not for the benefit of the child or the patient but for the smooth functioning of the institution. There is now a movement, started in St. Christopher's Hospice in England, to encourage children to visit and interact with dying patients. This is good for the dying because they are not cut off from the world and can express their feelings and good-byes in an atmosphere of love and community. It is good for the children because they are participating in a part of life. Children can become familiar with the realities of dying rather than being left with only their imaginations.

In the present care of the dying in most hospitals, children will not be permitted to visit unless parents work out special arrangements. Nursing homes are generally more flexible in their visitation rules. It is worth the trouble to find ways to get children in. A cooperative nurse, physician, or chaplain often can arrange for the rest of the staff to "look the other way" if we bring children on the floor. If we feel strongly about the child's being able to see the loved one this one last time and don't think we'll get hospital cooperation, we can act determinedly and firmly when taking the child past the front desk, which is usually the place where we will be stopped. Hospital rules can almost always be relaxed if someone of higher authority than a desk clerk gives permission. One of the authors secreted her three children (ages seven to twelve) up a side stairway so they could visit their dying grandmother, and their being able to see their grandmother for the last time would have been worth any trouble that came (but none did!). If it is in any way possible, the person can be brought in a wheelchair or movable bed to the lobby or outside the hospital on warm days.

Usually there are times when the dying will have good days, and these may be good times to plan a visit with the children. When we visit with young children, it is a good idea for them to have something specific to do or bring—a gift they have made, artwork from school, or food they have helped to make. The attention span of a child is short, so this should not be a long visit. Children above ten can interact naturally with the dying person. It helps if there are no secrets about the impending death, so the dying person and the child can say what is in their hearts at this time, knowing it may be the last. This will help to make the visit most meaningful for the child and the person who is dying. Adults who are dying may want to protect the child from that knowledge, because it is human nature to want to shield children from sadness and unhappiness. The dying person can be allowed to deny the seriousness of the illness to the child if he or she so chooses. For some, these moments with children are times of great warmth and joy in youth that do not have to be tinged with thoughts of death, when all other moments seem to be.

I am able to talk about death easily with my child, but I see a very negative response to the subject from my spouse. How do I handle the situation?

Children pick up fears from parents, but they pick up healthy attitudes as well. Parents need to remember that children are also individuals in their own right and are not totally structured by the parenting they get. When we offer them honest answers, allow them free expression of emotions, and enable them to think their ideas through, we are helping them form realistic, healthy attitudes toward death. Children can adopt whichever stance on death is most comfortable for them.

When our spouse has difficulty discussing death, we cannot demand that our partner change. The coming to terms with the problematic death experiences has to be a decision of each individual person, for the difficult self-examination needed takes a strong commitment. Further, we will not help our spouse by accusations, verbalized or silent, about his or her attitude. If we feel strongly that our spouse's response to death is hurting the child, perhaps we can enlist additional support or confirmation of our feelings by talking with the school counselor or some other mental health professional. Other skilled professionals can offer suggestions for working out specific family problems for the best interests of the child and the family as a whole—suggestions that we, as participants in the problem, would have difficulty seeing.

When shall I take my child to funerals, and what should I expect of the child?

It is possible to take a child as young as seven to a funeral. The child must be prepared in advance for what will be seen, how people might be behaving emotionally, and what rituals will take place. Children around seven or eight can be expected to sit reasonably well at a funeral service or mass for about thirty minutes. The adult in charge of the child should try to maintain a close physical presence to reassure the child and answer questions. Some advance provision should be made with another adult in the event that the child has to leave the funeral service before it is over or if the child does not accompany family members to the cemetery. The child should know this other person and that there is permission to leave early. In the case of the death of a parent, it is strongly advised that children as young as three be taken to the funeral to view the body *briefly* or to be part of the funeral setting for a few minutes. In our experience, whenever the death of a parent has occurred and the children are very young, unless they have some memory of the funeral and the body, the children never believe that the parent is dead. As adults, these children continue to search emotionally for their fathers or mothers throughout their lives, even to the extent of creating fantasies to explain the mother's or father's absence.

The child at the funeral service is basically an observer, although he or she may want to participate in familiar religious rituals. The child should *not* be forced to go up to the casket or touch the body in any way, even though others may be doing so. If a child does not wish to attend a funeral, he or she should not be coerced. The parent may wish to discuss the child's feelings about not going to find out why the child is apprehensive. If a child consistently refuses to attend appropriate family funerals over the years, this might be a warning that the child is having trouble with fears about death. Sometimes taking a group of children to visit the funeral chapel when no funeral is being conducted is all that is necessary to get over an initial reluctance due to a fear of unfamiliar surroundings. Most funeral directors are happy to explain things to children.

The adolescent is especially comforted at a funeral if there is some sense of usefulness. Teenagers can act as ushers and pallbearers whenever appropriate. Older children should be encouraged to offer a brief eulogy or prayer during the funeral service of a close family member.

Some parents do not want their children to attend funerals when the parents know that the adults will be visibly upset and unable to look after the children as they might wish. We do not feel that this is a good reason to exclude children from funerals. Adults provide models for grieving for children who need model behavior to help them become adults. Open display of emotion at a death is a good message to children who know that losses really hurt but don't know how to express that hurt publicly. Children need to see that men can cry when they are sad. Sharing sad feelings, for adults and children alike, is a more supportive and caring experience than grieving alone. If family members—because of a need to reflect and recuperate—seclude themselves from one another, this too can be explained to children who themselves may need the same "distancing." During the grief process at the time of mourning, it is important to remember that children cannot sustain feelings of grief as long as adults can. Children may mourn in interrupted periods of time, separated by hours, days, and weeks from the actual death. They may cry one minute and ask to go out to play the next. This is normal behavior for children, and adults should not expect grown-up behavior or the depths of adult grief from a child.

Children from ages seven to eleven may be more fascinated with the mechanics of the funeral director's tasks and the phsyical aspects of body disposal than with the emotional aspects of the funeral. This does not reflect a lack of feeling but a developmental stage in the child's life. Parents should not insist upon certain external signs of grief from children and should be understanding of their natural curiosity. The most outstanding characteristic of adolescent grief is the intense emotionality with which it is expressed. For example, crying may be bitter and prolonged and followed by the release of embarrassed laughter. Defending themselves against the outpouring of emotions that adolescents perceive as childlike may lead to the presentation of a rigid, stoic exterior that masks the inner turmoil.

How do I handle the topic of suicide and its occurrence?

When a suicide occurs, it is a natural inclination for the family to want to conceal the fact from outsiders and not to talk about it much among themselves. If the suicide has taken place outside the family circle, the child under eleven may be shielded from the specific details surrounding the death. Because young children express curiosity about "what is dead?" and do not comprehend the finality of death, we would not want them to experiment with any suicidal behaviors just to see what would happen (i.e., "What would happen if I jumped off the bridge or fell in front of a train?"). Young children often have romantic fantasies about death that we do not want to encourge. Information about the suicide should be conveyed when the child is old enough to understand the causality and finality of death and when the child can understand the parameters of mental illness or depression (usually about eleven or twelve). If the child begins to understand from family conversations and nonverbal communication that there is something different about this death, we might as well tell the child straightforwardly rather than have the information pieced together haphazardly and perhaps incorrectly. The child over eleven is usually old enough to understand the suicidal act. It is very important to stress that the person was not thinking clearly at the time of the suicide because of unhappiness, illness, or the like and that specially trained people can help others so they don't die when they feel unhappy or unloved, if the helpers are told of the bad feelings when they first occur.

Sometimes the suicide is another child. Suicides among children and teenagers are attributed to feelings of being unappreciated, disintegration of the family unit, fear of failure, or feelings of anger and wanting to punish the family. Frequently, poor grades, unfulfilled parental standards, unsatisfactory peer relationships, and uncertainty about developing sexuality will cause the twelve-to-thirteen-year-old to consider suicide seriously as he or she faces the unknown world of high school. Another crisis time for the adolescent is the senior year of high school, when separation from the family often takes place and significant decisions about impending autonomy and life choices must be made. Romantic notions of death ("The kids will all talk about me when I'm gone." "My parents will be sorry they weren't nicer to me." "What excitement my death will cause.") may provide the rationale for the method or setting used in the suicide plan. When talking to a teenager about the suicide of another, the teenager must be told that there was little, if anything, he or she could have done to prevent the suicide. The normal, almost automatic, response to suicide is a feeling of guilt on the part of the living that there was something that could have been done to prevent the death. "If only I had been more attentive," or "If only I hadn't turned him down for that date"; feelings like this reflect guilt and a feeling of responsibility for the death as well as the notion that a single individual's behavior would have made the difference between life and death for the suicide. This fallacy must be exposed—no one person was responsible for the suicidal feelings that caused the death, certainly not a person who was not intimately connected with the deceased. Studies suggest that the moment of suicide seems to be one of being overwhelmed by emotion.

Case histories indicate that children whose parents have committed suicide are more strongly disposed than other children to suicidal thoughts and gestures. If a parent or sibling commits suicide, perhaps it is best for the surviving adults and children to seek supportive counseling immediately as a family, so that feelings of being "doomed" or seeing suicide as an inevitable alternative to confrontation with life crises can be avoided. Parents and siblings are models for the family, even if the model is one we wish the children would not emulate.

If the suicide is that of an aged person who was ill, very often the official report of the death will focus solely on the physical illness. It's all right to say to a child,

"Grandma was so sick that she didn't have any fun living any more," and wait until the child asks further questions. Children become confused and frightened by suicide when the adults with whom they are in communication are confused and frightened themselves. Children will trust and accept adult communications if the adult is comfortable and can accept what is being said to the child.

When a suicide occurs, the death must be fully accepted and mourned, just as with any other death. Because of the social stigma attached to the suicidal act, too often families bury their feelings about the death along with the dead. It is folly to pretend that the person never existed or that the injury done to the family is so outrageous that the person may not be openly remembered. Such family behavior will affect the survivors adversely and may cause long-lasting psychological damage to the child. If a child knows that trust exists somewhere in the family so that problems and negative feelings can be empathically shared, then the need for suicidal gestures by the child will greatly diminish. The child who knows that questions about suicide will be honestly and reassuringly answered will not be frightened by it.

Our family pet is sick and old. It will either die or have to be euthanized soon. I know the family is very attached to our pet. How should I handle this?

Many of the college students we teach recall a pet's death as a most significant experience of death. We need to be sensitive to how the pet's death will affect the children in the family. For very young children, insensitivity may raise emotional problems that are not necessary. When one of our children was three, we hastily flushed a dead goldfish down the toilet and for the next month were forced to talk about that goldfish at least three times a day, as well as face a regression in bowel training. If we had thought a while, we would have put the fish in a box and buried it in the yard, so at least the discussions could more easily have led to death in general and the natural cycle of decomposition; and the toilet would not have become a burial place to be avoided by the child.

With children up to six or seven, the death of a pet raises mostly the question of what happened. They are familiar with the pet's activity, and if it does not move or respond, they now learn the difference between life and death. When we dispose of the body, they have to confront the question of "Where is my pet now?" There are basic intellectual questions about death that the young child is capable of understanding in a concrete way. If we use the pet's death constructively, this can become an educational experience. There is also an emotional side to the death of the pet for young children. They will be frightened, sad, or angry but sometimes without adequate ideas or words to express and understand their feelings. We can give them the words by saying what we think they are feeling (or what we are feeling about the loss of the pet) and give them permission to express these feelings of grief. Some children's books like *The Tenth Good Thing About Barney* or *The Dead Bird* can be used to advantage by parents in these circumstances. By having parents read the story with them, the children can learn that they are not alone in feeling the way they do when they experience a loss.

Children over eight can understand the difference between their attachments to animals and their attachments to people. They can also understand the difference between animal death and human death. But though they can understand the difference, they will still have strong feelings of grief if the pet has been an important part of their childhood. When children have had no experience with human death, the death of a pet can be a good time for parents to talk about the meaning of loss and to reassure the child that feelings he or she may have are shared and normal.

Our mistake of throwing the goldfish into the toilet should be a warning to parents to think carefully about disposing of the pet's body. There is a very therapeutic aspect to digging a hole in the yard and burying the animal or carrying the animal in a dignified fashion to the veterinarian for cremation. If we bury the pet, we can reminisce about the pet's life and talk about what will happen to the body—that it will become part of the ground and provide nourishment for plants. Children usually want to make some kind of marker for the grave, and this can be a very helpful activity for them. Children from religious backgrounds may want to plan a service for the pet. Ritual serves as a good outlet, for it channels feelings and gives children structures within which they can later fit the experience of human death.

When our children are young, there is a tendency to try to deny the loss by immediately replacing the pet with another. This does not take seriously the child's attachment to the pet that died. Some parents have had very bad experiences when they simply went out and bought another animal. If we think replacing the pet is a good idea, we should include the child in the discussion and if the decision is made to get another, the child should participate in the selection.

Euthanasia for pets often is a hard matter for adults to face and is even harder for children. To be sure, the moral dilemmas surrounding active euthanasia for animals are not of the same order as decisions we often must make about human death, but young children may not be able to tell the difference. Yet the need to end the suffering of a dog or cat is a good opportunity to introduce children to the ethical and humanitarian questions of life and death. There is no reason to hide decisions to euthanize from children of any age, though as parents we should take the responsibility for the decision with children under eight and let children over eight be part of the decision-making process. In the discussion, we can consider the relative age of the pet to human age, the probable future course of the pet's illness, and the possibilities and costs for treatment, the nature of suffering, and the part death plays in the life cycle. With younger children, a week may be enough time between the introduction of the topic and the time the pet is taken away. With older children, if they are to be part of the decision-making process, there may be several weeks of discussion before the matter is settled. Sometimes parents must do what's best for the pet, even though the children have not yet accepted the parents' decision. It is important to keep the discussion of the issue open until the child has finished with the problem.

When one of our family pets was dying of a congenital heart defect after nine loving years as companion to the family's teenagers, the youngest daughter (then fourteen) refused to accept the need to euthanize the pet. It was agreed that she would make the decision as to when the pet was to be euthanized, so long as she was aware of his suffering. Night after night she listened to his labored breathing until one Sunday when she cradled him in her blanket and said, "I'm ready to go now." A forced decision would not have allowed her to come to this kind of growth and insight that she would need as an adult. We both cried all the way to the veterinary hospital.

How do I recognize when my child is grieving?

Grief is the process by which the human mind comes to terms with loss. As such, grief is not a specific emotion like depression or anger but rather a constellation of feelings that can be expressed by many behaviors, emotions, and thoughts and can be resolved by many modes and symbols. To understand the breadth of behavior possible, let us compare grief to love, which is also not a single emotion but a response to an emotional attachment. Adolescents in love may be shy, aggressive, confused, awed, highly verbal, silent, physically sick, or feel like "dancing on clouds." Grieving children can express their grief in just as many ways. They may have physical symptoms, engage in hostile activities toward others, deny that anything has changed, idealize the dead, have free-floating anxiety, feel guilty, or panic completely. Children, especially those under eight, commonly do not express and identify their grief verbally but speak to us in symbolic language, using fantasy play or acting out feelings for which they have no words.

When communications have been open throughout experiences of dying and death, where parents have included the children in the rituals the culture provides to express grief, and whenever the parents have been able to satisfactorily resolve their own grief, children are able to mourn their loss with the adults and also get on with the business of living. As adults we sometimes confuse our reaction to a death with the child's reaction and project what we are feeling onto the child. For example, when we feel angry but cannot admit it to ourselves, we may interpret our child's behavior as if the child were demonstrating our anger when in fact the child is not the one who is angry.

Once we become aware of the dynamics of projection, we can look at the child's behavior as it really is. Children do grieve but often in different ways than adults. Most often the child does not know that he or she is grieving, just that there are confusing and troublesome feelings that he or she has no words for. The hallmark for identifying possible grief at work in the child is to identify *uncharacteristic* behavior for that child and for the developmental stage of that child. Any marked change in the child after a significant death or loss is enough evidence to suspect that it is a grief response.

> Peter, whose older brother had died, began burying toys in one corner of the sandbox while playing there. Gradually he buried so many toys that he had no room left to play. One day his father was working in the yard and suggested the boy play in the sandbox, and the child said he couldn't because it was full of toys for his brother to play with. The father stopped and listened to the symbolic language of the child and thought about what it meant. The toys were being buried in the sand just as the dead brother was buried in the ground. Perhaps this was a way Peter believed he could communicate and play with his brother. A few days later, he talked to his son about the dead brother, telling him that the dead child didn't need to play with toys. The parents then gave the little boy a picture of his brother to keep in his room. For several weeks after that, the child chatted with his dead brother while he played, slowly bringing the toys out of the sand. Gradually, talking to his brother diminished as the parents spent extra time with the child and shared memories of the dead child more openly.

No two people are alike in grieving. Since children
under eight often do not have the words to express themselves, we may need to figure out what the symbolic behavior means and then join the child in the symbolism, as
the father did by hanging the photograph in the child's
room, or encourage the child to verbalize with our help.
Older children are more likely to be verbal, but they too
can use symbolic behavior and language.

> Ellen, seventeen years old, blamed herself for not loving her
> father enough and thought her lack of attention to him caused his
> death. She began dating boys who were abusive, and her sexual
> behavior with them was self-destructive. The mother was angry
> at first, but her anger only drove the girl to more destructive
> behavior. When the mother perceived the symbolism of her
> daughter's actions, she told their clergyman what she thought
> was happening. He spoke with Ellen at several meetings, and she
> was able to break off the harmful relationships and go back to her
> old group of friends. The clergyman was able to convince the girl
> that she had been a loving daughter to her father and thereby rid
> her of the need for punishment by men. Because of the nature of
> his religious role, he was also able to expiate her guilt and assure
> her of her father's love and forgiveness for real problems between
> them.

I am dying. How can I now help my child?

It is not simply we who are dying, but a part of everyone
we know will die with us. This is especially true of our
children under eight who have very little sense of identity
apart from us. Yet it is hard to think about others now, for
our minds are full of very self-centered anxieties, and our
bodies often call attention only to themselves. At times we
can rationally accept our diagnosis, but at other times we
just want to forget what is happening and live as best we
can—as if it isn't true. When we are trying to forget about

it, we hope others will, too, so we are not ready to pick up the cues from our children that they are ready for us to help them. When we do accept that we are dying, we want our family to be close to us, warmly supporting the tentative peace we sometimes feel or comforting the terror we face at the possibility of our nonexistence. But we often find that it is just at that time they withdraw, either because they are angry at us for dying or simply because they cannot face the reality of our death at the same time we do.

Within the chaotic sense of changing feelings and missed timings, we can help our children most by including them as much as possible in the process through which we are going and including the fact of death as much as possible into the family life. This means that when we find out about our illness, we share what we know about the future course of the disease, our eventual physical limitations, and the possibilities of treatment. The hardest things to face are those we do not know. This is true of us and of our children. Young children will not perceive gradual changes in the dying adult and will continue to make demands, not understanding why they are not met. Children need to be prepared for what will happen, and it is no favor to protect them now so they will find out both about our death and our lying to them at the same time. The facts should be presented fully and in as simple language as the child can comprehend. Open, trustworthy communication allows the family system to adapt gradually to the eventual absence of the terminally ill family member. It may be helpful for older children to talk to the physician in charge of treatment. If there are decisions to be made about life-prolonging measures or funeral arrangements, children above the age of eleven or twelve can, to the extent they are willing, participate in those discussions. If there are also decisions to be made about care of the children after we die, those decisions should be discussed with the children, so they do not feel that their whole lives are out of their hands.

We also need to share with our children the meaning impending death has for us as well as the meaning of our life. This is not easy, for in the various stages of grieving for ourselves, we may come up with different answers. With younger children, this may mean explaining personal beliefs so they can incorporate these beliefs into coping behaviors and later belief systems of their own. With older children, the process will probably involve long discussions as they try to make sense out of this death in the context of their lives.

We should not try to anticipate how others will respond to our death, for each person—adult and child—must find his or her own way to come to terms with it. Some children will need to withdraw from us for a time while they get their bearings. As hard as it is, we have to give them that freedom. For some teenagers, that withdrawal is permanent. They have been in the process of moving away from us and finding other adults or peers who have become their primary reference group. When they hear of our impending death, they may find it easier to simply accelerate that movement rather than to redevelop a close tie with us that will soon be broken. As a result, some teenagers will resent the additional household responsibilities our sickness now puts on them. But we need not blame every bit of problematic relationship on the death. After all, just being a teenager is often enough to make a child hard to get along with.

As the children begin to accept the fact that we will

die soon, some of them will for a time feel as though it is our fault that we are dying and blame us for leaving them. Others will feel as if they are responsible in some way for our impending death. If we keep the channels of communication open, such feelings can be part of our ongoing discussions and can be resolved.

We feel that at least at our death, everything ought to go smoothly. But death is part of life and so is seldom ideal. We can finish our business, but if we do die without finishing all our tasks, we can hope that we have transmitted the best we have to offer of ourselves to those we have to leave behind, so they can find their way in the world.

When should I talk to my children about death?

Situations concerning death are part of all life and occur on a regular basis in the lives of children. There is no need to wait for some special time, for the subject of death will come up spontaneously in many discussions, such as "Why doesn't the goldfish swim anymore?" or "What happened to the flower?" Death is an inevitable part of the lives of families, and few children are unaware of the effects of a death on family members, no matter how peripheral that death may be to their own interests and relationships. All these times, and others, are appropriate times to talk about death and dying. We must be careful, however, not to jump at these opportunities with a fully loaded arsenal of information that may be more than the child can understand or assimilate at once. Just as we parcel out sex information to the curious child at the level the child can understand and answer the question being asked rather than our own questions, we do the same with information about death.

When someone the child knows dies, or when a teacher is absent because he or she had to attend a funeral, the question on the child's mind may very well be about what is happening. At that time an explanation of the events with information about death can be given. This explanation can include the fact that many people are gathering for the funeral or at the house of the mourners and why, that a person has died and what he or she died from, what will be done with the body, and whatever religious belief about death is held by the child's family or the family of the deceased.

By the time a child goes to kindergarten, parents will probably have had several natural opportunities to talk about death with their child, so that at his or her own cognitive and emotional level, the child understands what death is, what happens socially when a death occurs, and that death is part of life.

If we have avoided talking about death with our children when they were younger, there is no good reason for us to suddenly panic and sit them down in a quiet place and in hushed, solemn tones explain it all right now. Even with older children, it is best to talk openly of death at home as the occasion demands, at the change from fall to winter, when someone dies, when a funeral procession passes, or when there is a significant public death. If we find that the older child is voicing some misconceptions, this can become an occasion for fruitful discussion and frank, loving interchange of ideas.

The answer, then, to when should we talk to our children about death is simply whenever the world, as they experience and question it, includes death.

I cannot talk about death at all to anyone. How do I prevent my child from inheriting my fears?

If we try to cover up our emotional response to death, our children will understand that there is something special but unknown and dangerous about death, for their most innocent comments will bring an emotional response from us that is not consistent with the comments or questions they raised. It is therefore impossible for our fears not to affect our children in some way if we try to pretend that we don't have them.

We have two options. The first is to take on the hard yet ultimately rewarding job of facing our fears, finding out where they came from, what experiences in our past they are connected to, and how they function in the course of our lives. We can make a decision to stop feeling the way we do about death. All adults need to examine their emotional relationship with death if they are to educate children about it. An outline for such a self-examination is provided in Chapter 5. If, after thoughtful exploration of the issues raised in that chapter, we are still left with unreasonable fears or feelings, perhaps we should seek professional help. The strong feelings we have about death are not accidental. They are there for some reason, perhaps unknown to us at the moment, but they can be resolved and our comfort restored. Some of the strong emotions surrounding death may be connected to other problematic areas in our lives—fear of separation or of our own aggressive impulses or something else. If we decide to take the option of confronting our fears directly, we should be prepared for some major psychological insights. The advantage of this option—painful as it might be—is that at its conclusion, we can communicate our whole-some relationship with death to our children, and they can learn from the model we set for them.

The other option is to openly admit to our children that we have a problem in talking about death, that it is our problem, and that they can get little help from us because of it. The way we do this is to state clearly to the child that we have strong feelings about death that we are not yet comfortable sharing with anyone. For example, we might say: "I am really uncomfortable every time I think about death," or "I haven't been able to figure out what death is all about myself, so I have trouble talking about it. Maybe you can get some help from —————— [Daddy, Grandma, Aunt Sally]." What we should try to do is help the child to differentiate between his or her experiences and perceptions related to death and our own unresolved fears and concerns. We can then put our child into contact with someone who can provide answers to the questions the child has—someone with whom the child can com-municate comfortably.

What do I say to my child if he or she asks if I will die someday?
By all means, say yes—after all, that's the fact of the mat-ter. For the preschool child, the question may be merely a curious one—"If other people die, will you die, too?" For most children, questions about the death of parents are connected with fear of separation from those on whom they are dependent and with the fear that the aggressive feelings they harbor against parents may result in actual harm to the parents. The feeling of magical omnipotence in younger children is especially frightening when they imagine their fantasies of acting out their negative emo-

tions toward parental figures. For children of all ages, the answer should be accompanied by the reassurance that no child can cause a death and that we do not expect to die but expect to be able to stay with our children for as long as we are needed by them. This answer presumes reasonable good health for the parents. If, however, we are very sick or hospitalized often, the young children may connect our illness with death from things they have read or television programs they have seen, and an honest, hopeful answer must be offered if we are chronically ill. We can, if the young child questions us fearfully, give what we understand to be a realistic evaluation of our chances of dying at this time. This puts possible death into the realm of reality and out of the sphere of the imagination. What our children imagine is more frightening than what they know. The question of parental death among latency and prepubescent children may be one of curiosity or feelings of egocentrism together with the earlier concerns of the younger child. Whereas the young child fears loss and abandonment, the older child may be wondering, "What will I do?" and "What will happen to me?" if a parent dies. It is not unusual for a child to ask a parent if he or she would remarry after the death of the spouse, and that question is based on the child's imagining what it would be like to have a different father or mother and wanting not to be different from other families. The major difference may be that the older child is less ready to transfer loyalties. The older teenager is deeply concerned about the extent to which he or she might be called upon to take over the role and responsibilities of the dead or dying parent. The "middle-aged" child frequently voices very practical monetary concerns or home-management problems. The younger child fears loss of emotional support, food, and physical protection. We can sometimes see in the fantasies of older children some dissatisfaction with the present world—fantasies of mother marrying a professional football player or a movie star, fantasies of an imaginary father with no bad qualities. On the other hand, the image of the bad stepmother seems to be a rather primordial one, so imagining another mother is more often a threatening thought, although it is possible to wish for a mother who doesn't ask children to clean up their room so often. With older teenagers, the question may also reflect a concern about knowing what to do in the event of a death or their questioning of their ability to handle adult problems without parental guidance. Sometimes talking and dreaming about the death of a parent are ways of working out the underlying negative feelings of the teenager toward the adult or ways of achieving separation and individuation, which is a process so central to the adolescent years. We do our children no service if we foster notions of our immortality. Rather, it is better to reassure the child that we hope and expect to be able to raise them safely to adulthood, and then we will be satisfied that we have completed our parental tasks.

FURTHER READING

BARNES, MARION J., "The Reactions of Children in Adolescence to the Death of a Parent or Sibling," in *The Child and Death*, ed. Olle Jane Sahler. St. Louis, Mo.: C.V. Mosby Co., 1978.

BLUEBOND–LANGNER, MYRA, *The Private Worlds of Dying Children*. Princeton, N.J.: Princeton University Press, 1978.

BURTON, LINDY, *Care of the Child Facing Death*. London: Routledge & Kegan Paul, 1974.

EASSON, WILLIAM M., "Management of the Dying Child," *Journal of Clinical Child Psychology*, 3:2 (Summer 1974), 25–27.

————, *The Dying Child: The Management of the Child or Adolescent Who Is Dying*. Springfield, Ill.: Charles C Thomas, 1970.

FURMAN, ERNA, *A Child's Parent Dies*. New Haven, Conn.: Yale University Press, 1974.

GLASER, BARNEY, and ANSELM STRAUSS, *Awareness of Dying*. Chicago: Aldine, 1966.

GROLLMAN, EARL A., *Talking About Death: A Dialogue Between Parent and Child*. Boston: Beacon Press, 1970.

HAGIN, ROSA, and CAROL G. CORWIN, "Bereaved Children," *Journal of Clinical Child Psychology*, 3:2 (Summer 1974), 39–41.

IRISH, JERRY, *A Boy Thirteen: Reflections on Death*. Philadelphia: Westminster, 1975.

JACKSON, EDGAR, *Telling a Child About Death*. New York: Channel Press, 1966.

MARTINSON, IDA M., *Home Care for the Dying Child*. New York: Appleton-Century-Crofts, 1976.

MORIARTY, DAVID M., *The Loss of Loved Ones*. Springfield, Ill.: Charles C Thomas, 1967.

SCHIFF, HARRIET S., *The Bereaved Parent*. New York: Crown, 1977.

WILLIS, DIANE J., "The Families of Terminally Ill Children: Symptomatology and Management," *Journal of Clinical Child Psychology*, 3:2 (Summer 1974), 32–33.

People die all the time, but somehow when teachers get involved in teaching about death, they find themselves much more sensitive to death and problems related to death. We find ourselves confronted with three kinds of situations: (1) when we help individual students who are anxious about their own death and/or deaths of significant others; (2) when a child learns about a death; and (3) when we acknowledge deaths that are significant to the school community (or to society as a whole) for which a communal response is therapeutic. Like death itself, these situations find us; we do not have to seek them out. If we use these situations as learning experiences, we can educate in ways that will have the most lasting effects.

Coping with Death and Dying in the School Setting

Chapter **4**

STUDENTS TROUBLED BY DEATH

We ought to think for a moment about our students and the years in which they have lived. We can try to imagine ourselves at their age right now. They grow up in a time when the sight of natural death has been banished from everyday living but in a time when the nuclear bomb and the Nazi holocaust have made death more familiar than at any time since the plague of the fourteenth century. They see violent,death portrayed on film, TV physicians performing miraculous cures for those deserving to live, and death as a punishment for evil deeds. Science promises a cure for human suffering. The media promote happiness as an ultimate goal and right, yet the students know that death is real, that sometimes death involves suffering, and that death can cause unhappiness. The concrete faith of the grandparents about death and justice has not always been successfully transmitted to the grandchildren, so they face death without the heritage or familiarity that would have been theirs in another day. The caring neighborhood is passing, and the extended family may be far away. The religious rituals of death are often reserved for family alone. When death and its attendant anxieties occur, our students want to do something but don't know what or how. When their fears about personal death become conscious, they are afraid to share these fears, so they don't know if they are appropriate. When they experience a death, only a few close friends may know about it, so they walk the school halls with an important reality that is essentially private. Or conversely, they may feel singled out by exaggerated attention to the death that makes them feel embarrassed and on public display. Friends won't tell jokes or laugh in front of the student or may avoid meeting the student because of discomfort over what to say. The student then feels isolated from normal contacts and has little interaction with friends that is appropriate. There is also the seeming cruelty of young children who do not accept the finality of death, so they make jokes or taunt one another when death occurs as a way of relieving their anxiety about death fears.

And then we introduce open talk about death and dying into the classroom. Sometimes during a discussion or after a thought-provoking reading or movie, we see tears or a look of distraction on a student's face that cannot be boredom. When this happens, we often find that it is we who are not paying attention to what is going on. In the back of our minds, we wonder if we really did the right thing teaching about death—look how upsetting it is. As the class continues, we weigh whether we should just hope the student drops by to see us or if we should ask if we can help. Most of us who teach about death find that some students seek us out for private conversation. They often begin with a clumsy excuse, but somehow we know that they are really there to talk about something very important to them. As we listen, many of us feel very inadequate and clumsy ourselves.

Grave problems can arise when we deny the seriousness of the subject and the depth of feeling that it generates. We know of a situation in which the mother of a high school senior girl had died after a surgical procedure. The death was unexpected—the mother was comparatively young. The family sought psychological counseling not long after the death. After a few sessions, the father, who had initiated the counseling, said he was OK and he thought everyone else was, too. Life went on uneventfully for the family. Nine months later, an English teacher at the high school decided to offer a four-week minicourse on "Death and Dying" to his students. The students were asked to write a paper on the subject on anything of interest. The girl wrote a lengthy paper about the experience of her mother's death. She sought out the teacher repeatedly to talk with him, but apart from praising the depth of the paper, the teacher did not want to talk any more about it. A week later the girl took a drug overdose; fortunately, she was discovered in time to be saved. She then began receiving further psychological help to work through her delayed grief reaction to her mother's death. There are two points to be considered in this example. First, people don't always work through their grief when they're "supposed to," and second, the girl's teacher (who had known of the mother's death) should have been alert to the girl's turmoil and steered her to some kind of counseling. He should have realized that the subject he had presented as a literature topic for four weeks was more powerful than most school subjects and potentially upsetting to his students. Perhaps his lack of response was indicative of his own fears about death.

As responsible teachers for this subject matter, we must be prepared to follow through with students who seem to need extra time for private talks. If the problem seems pervasive throughout the student's life, perhaps a consultation or joint meeting (teacher, student, and family) with the school counselor or psychologist might be helpful at this point. We should trust our instincts to alert us to something wrong. Getting help for the studnet *now* may prevent future years of sadness and limited functioning. Death anxieties are common causes of later pathological behavior. We may be able to facilitate counseling for the entire family if needed, if we can recognize problems that can occur during bereavement and get immediate help.

Our students have thought about their own deaths and have faced the deaths of significant persons just as adults do. Like many people, they have been isolated with their thoughts and feelings by our culture's basic denial of death. It should not surprise us that when we introduce death topics into the classroom, the problems and feelings the students have repressed come to the fore. If their thoughts and feelings come out so strongly that they make us uncomfortable, we need to remember two things: First, as their thoughts have rolled around in the subconscious, they have been lumped together with other strong material that also stays repressed; and second, most students have strong feelings that they have not yet learned to express "politely."

The Student as Mourner

The first thing to know is that we can handle most crises or problems—we have most of what it takes to serve our students well. We are human—we face death ourselves—and we may have suffered losses that are significant to us (divorce, loss of a job, a pet, death, and so on). We can offer those troubled by death our own humanity and our own experience as we face death and mourn our losses together.

Of course it's scary. But the unknown is always scary,

and death brings us in contact with the unknown. We have worked privately with many students in our classes, and each time it is with heart in mouth and echoes of past pain. We can give them all we have—and watch the healing process flourish in the healthy atmosphere of human contact. Don't send them to someone else unless their functioning is clearly inappropriate and should be handled by a professional with psychological training. Refusing to discuss appropriate anxieties and problems of everyday living only makes these problems seem bigger to the students and to us.

So what do we as educators and parents say? The answer is simple; we don't have to say anything at first—we *just listen* to the child. We must *make sure we hear what the student is saying!* This means first making sure that we hear what is said and not what we think he or she ought to have said. For example, the death of a parent might lead us to expect a student to feel abandoned, lonely, and sad, and we begin to respond to the student as if that is the case. But if we really listen, we might find that the student feels angry or guilty or relieved. The student's feelings may be very different from our own in the same situation. We can try to listen without judgment or expectation. What the studnet needs is an ear and an understanding face so all the thoughts, memories, and feelings can be shared. Many people do not really know what they feel before they hear themselves say it. When we hear themselves, they begin to understand what they are feeling and make sense out of that feeling as it relates to their thought or memory. Once the feeling is expressed in words, it does not have the power it had when it was formless; so somehow just saying and hearing it makes people feel better. So what we can do is to encourage students to talk—"Tell me about it" or "Can I help?"—and then listen closely, trying to understand just what they are feeling. Empathic listening will help them talk more.

Sometimes this means listening to memories. When someone we love has died, we have to sever the bond that once held us, but at the same time we want to hold on to the relationship. We are literally formed by primary relationships to which we feel wholly committed. The act of remembering makes the dead part of our present in a different way. Before the death, we acted as if there was a future with that person; after the death, we seek to preserve the past relationship through memory.

Not all memories are pleasant; some are terrible. These need to come out too. They are often laden with bitterness or guilt, so that as they are relived, the old feelings come out again. The trouble with such memories is that before we share and resolve them, we act and feel as if the events were in the present when they are not. If we can help students get the memories out and share them, the present can get some control over the events of the past. In other words, the student may say, "Yes, he did treat Mom and me badly, and I often wished he were dead. Now he is dead, and I know I didn't have anything to do with it, yet I feel guilty that I'm glad he's dead." The student can only make such a statement if the memories come out, helped by a listening ear and a nonjudgmental attitude. We can reassure the student that he or she has nothing to do with causing the death. We can point out that the anger we feel toward someone doesn't go away easily just because that person is dead—and that it's OK to feel relieved about the death and still have angry feelings.

As we listen, we hear other things besides memory. We hear feelings that start "if only." These are part of what Kübler–Ross calls the bargaining stage. It is a way of saying the death (or an impending death) would be more acceptable *if only* something were different: if only the student had been a more loving child, if only the death had been faster, if only a task had been completed. Sometimes such bargains can be made and kept. If the death is impending, there is still time to say the yet unspoken words or do some appropriate thing. If the death is past, there is still the opportunity to communicate with other family members or to finish tasks the dead person may have begun. But other times, we must live with life as incomplete and accept the death including the "if only." Like memories, these "if only" thoughts have more power before they are spoken than after they are said. Often the student will not realize what is so bothersome until in the course of talking, the words just come out, and then the troublesome feelings may go away spontaneously.

As we listen, we may also hear statements expressing feelings of abandonment and separation. The problem of separation is a major aspect of the child's relationship with death. We hear the lonely question of "Who will take care of me?" or perhaps the longing for reunion of "I want to die, too." And often we hear fears of the student's own death brought on by the death of another. All these are natural thoughts that do not indicate any psychotic quality. But the power of these fantasies only lasts as long as they remain inside the student's head. When we listen actively so that the fantasies come out and are shared, they lose their power and we—with the student—can put them in a realistic perspective.

As we listen, we try to put ourselves inside the other person in order to feel in ourselves what they are feeling—to empathize. Empathy is becoming one with the other person so that we know subjectively what they know subjectively. Sometimes empathy is difficult when people are very different from us in age, background, or personality. We should try not to project our own feelings, so that as we listen we can experience the feelings they have. We use our humanity to understand their humanity. We have two advantages in our empathic feelings that we can use to help students. First, we have a wider range of experience, so we can find words and analogies by which we can help define their feelings: "It sounds to me as if you are feeling. . . . ," followed by your own words that try to express what they are having trouble putting into words; or, "I remember feeling that way when . . . and it felt like. . . ." Second, we are not as immediately involved as they, so we can put feelings and thoughts into the perspectives of time and other parts of their lives.

The Teacher's Response

Now we can begin to ask the question, "What do I say?" Again, the answer is simple—we can say what we feel. Death makes us feel alone and cut off from other people. When we share feelings with one another—real feelings, not platitudes—we know we are not alone. If we feel sorry, we can say we're sorry; if we feel bewildered, we can say we're bewildered; if we're angry, we can say so. Tears are a good way to share humanity. If we feel like crying with the student, the sadness the student feels is shared, so it's not so lonely. If the student cries and we do not, we can give permission, "Go ahead and cry—it's all right." Permission may be necessary, since so many strong feelings are labeled as being publicly unacceptable, and some children are taught in the family to hide negative emotions and only show a pleasant (or stoic) face to the world.

Sometimes students will bring out negative emotions in us, and these can be shared. We must be careful, however, that although we feel impatient or angry with students, we let them know we accept them as people. It is just that we cannot accept how they are responding or what they are doing to themselves. So when we share our negative feelings, we need to do it within an expression of concern for the student.

> Ann, fifteen years old, was repeatedly absent from class, inappropriately dressed for school, impudent, and disliked by students and teachers alike. Ann still appeared to be in mourning eight years after her father's death. She could not think about him without feelings of sadness and anger that his death had changed her life in so many ways. Her mother had remarried and the family had moved to a new neighborhood, and she had a baby brother from this new marriage that she had to help care for. Ann's problems seemed to express themselves in her sexuality. She was extremely promiscuous with males somewhat older than her peers. In counseling Ann, it was pointed out that she had used her father's death as a way to avoid taking responsibility for the destructive things she did to herself and others. Ann felt that if her father could desert her, then she was "no good," and she acted accordingly. Infantile behaviors Ann exhibited were explained as ways in which she refused to be an adult, so that she could still hold on to her childhood and her father's presence. Several sessions focusing on the meaning of her father's death helped Ann to stop punishing herself and led to more constructive relationships with her family and peers.

Beyond sharing feelings, we can also share our solutions to the student's problems. As people, we have coped with difficult times and problems. It helps our students to see that someone else has gone through a predicament like theirs and made it. We can help the student by sharing our own history. When a student has lost a parent, we can remember aloud the time we grieved over a significant loss. We can mention the things that helped—what somebody said or did, books we read, thoughts we found comforting. Young people are trying to find paths in the world for the feelings and thoughts they have. Our experience may not be exactly the same as theirs, but it can provide models for them. Sharing our own experience also takes away some of the loneliness the student feels. The student can know that where he is is a place someone else has been before. That takes some of the strangeness out of it.

We can share our solution to basic philosophical problems that death raises. Somehow we have developed ways of understanding life that help us to cope with the loss of others and our own mortality. If we label clearly that this is *our* way and not one that the student *must* follow, we can share our solution. It may be a rather well thought out life philosophy, or it may be religious convictions we hold that give meaning to life and death. It may be just a story the child can identify with or an insight we have about death. This is not an opportunity to preach or try to convert the student to our religious stance. Rather, it is an opportunity for one human being to share the meaning of life with another human being for whom the meaning of life has become problematic. That we share our life philosophy does not mean that we have reached a solution for ourselves that will last for all time. We say, "This is what makes sense to me at this point," and hope that through our help the student can find something that makes sense. Younger students (nursery–primary) may just need extra cuddling or reassurance of security and acceptance when they feel scared or sad.

A special word to teachers, counselors, and parents who think they might have a child who needs a level of help we can't provide.

When it becomes apparent that the problem the child is having with death is tied in with other behavioral or emotional problems that cause the child to function asocially, then it is time for teachers and counselors to recommend that the child be seen by a mental health professional and for the parents to take action. As we noted in Chapter 2, there is some research to indicate that at least among adolescents, those who have severe problems with death are likely to have other problems. This appears to be true of younger children as well. There are no absolute indications as to when a child needs outside help. When we see behaviors like regressive changes in bowel and bladder control, persistent sleep problems, excessive aggression, hyperactivity, extended loss of ability to concentrate, extended withdrawal into the self, continued regression into lower developmental levels of behavior, wild swings in emotion, or expression of thought that indicates a loss of contact with reality, then perhaps the child needs more help than we can give. Sometimes normal grief looks very much like mental illness, and we need to learn to be sensitive to the differences. We do not want to label a child as abnormal prematurely or unnecessarily. This places a difficult responsibility upon educators and parents, but as we come to understand the child in relation to death, we can exercise that responsibility better.

To summarize the points made in this part of the chapter:

— We can help children when they have problems with death.
— Listen and empathize.
— Respond with real feelings.
— Share personal experiences and life philosophy.
— Refer when necessary.

WHEN A CHILD LEARNS ABOUT A DEATH

The second situation that confronts us is when a child is at school and a family death occurs. It is not uncommon for students to be at school when a family learns of a death and wants to inform the student. The question is how should the student be told under these circumstances. It is probably best for the families of very young children (nursery–primary age) to ask the school to have the child ready to be picked up by a familiar person, so the child can be told within the family setting. It is important that the school office (that takes the message) and the teacher know exactly when this person is coming, so that the child does not have to be separated from normal school activities until the actual departure from school grounds. Other children in the class who ask about the child's sudden absence can be told that something sad has happened and that when the teacher has more information, it will be given to the class. Sudden news can be misleading, and the teacher often needs more facts than are available. When children of different ages and grades of the same family are in the same school, they should be gathered together for "telling about the death" so they can be with each other for comforting.

If the teacher or counselor is given this responsibility, here are some pointers gleaned from our experiences in "telling the news."

1. Take the student to a private place as quickly as possible. This kind of news travels fast, and the student should not overhear it accidentally. ("Overhearing the news" is a common occurrence, especially in hospitals and schools, and the bereaved may later resent that they received the information in this way.)

2. Be simple and direct in what is said, no matter what the child's age is. "Your father had a heart attack and he is dead." "Your brother was in a car accident and he is dead." Don't use euphemisms! *Don't* say, "Your father has expired" or "passed away." Euphemisms may be confusing to the student. Do not leave the student in doubt as to what has happened. Use the word *dead* or *died*. There is no ambiguity in it and no chance of misunderstanding. We do not want the student to have false hopes about the reality of the death. (Our own feelings right now are unimportant.) Respond to the student's behavior—don't be concerned with expressing sympathy and shock.

3. Do not go into details about how the death occurred. As an outsider, we may not know the details, and even if we think we do, this is something for the family members to share with one

another. Ultimately, "the story of the death" will become a family legend, and the student must share that reality as a family member. Whatever we say about the death in these first few moments may never be forgotten. If it is in conflict with what the student may find out later, it may cause difficulty in believing anything about the reality of the death. If we think back to whenever we have received shocking news, we can understand how important it is for accurate, clear-cut information to be simply transmitted.

After the student has heard the news, we need to respond appropriately to the student's needs:

1. People respond in many different ways to bad news. Speak quietly to the student, but do not expect a response at this time. The student may seem dazed, move woodenly, and feel chilled. The student may also appear to be behaving normally until the facts are intellectually processed, or the student may become very agitated physically (crying, screaming, angry denials, and so on).

2. Physical contact can be very helpful. We can hold hands, give a hug, or gently touch the student if we have a close enough relationship or it seems right at the time. In some cases, physical contact may be the only means of communication as the shock sets in. Some people resist personal contact when they find themselves in emotional trouble. They want to curl up inside themselves to hide and resent any intrusion. A student's need for this privacy should be respected, but the student should not be left alone. For the pubescent student, sexuality is related to death, and touching is associated with sexual feelings. Teachers need to be sensitive to these issues when working with students of the opposite sex.

3. Take the student to a quiet place to sit or lie down comfortably. (Stay with the student.) Offer something to drink—cola, juice, milk, or the like. Cover the student with a blanket or jacket, as this will feel comforting and will help to combat physical shock.

4. As time goes by, if the student remains completely silent, give the student permission to scream or cry or act out in some way. This

permission can be important, since it communicates the information that we are in control even if the student isn't, and therefore being out of control is OK. Phrases such as "It's OK to cry" or "I'd feel like screaming if I were you" are typical "permission" phrases.

5. After the student has ventilated some feelings, the words may begin to pour out. Just listen!! Let them come out and taper off. Maintain whatever physical contact the student is comfortable with, and reassure the student that she or he is OK. Remember that the situation the student faces may not be OK and that we do not have the power to change reality for this student.

6. Be genuine in emotional responses. If we want to cry with the student, it's OK. If we feel angry that this had to happen, we can recognize the feeling and express it. We may be able to help the student identify powerful yet confusing feelings that occur at these times. The adult can be a model of how to express grief, so hiding feelings does not help the student understand how to mourn appropriately.

7. Encourage the student to rest for a while. If we can't stay with the student, then we must arrange to have someone else take our place. When the student goes home, make sure he or she is accompanied by a familiar person.

The student may be absent for some time. When we see him or her again:

1. We shouldn't be surprised if the student avoids us afterwards for a while. The next time we see the student, we can be warm and positive but not overly inquisitive or overly possessive. We should not act significantly different than the way we have in the past toward the student. Bereaved students need to feel that they are basically the same persons and that although something in their lives may have changed, their relationships have not. We can be especially sensitive to the fact that other students may avoid or be overly solicitous toward a bereaved classmate, and we should do what we can to urge others to resume normal relationships.

2. If the student seeks us out at a later time, we can acknowledge our continued willingness to help. Don't assume that just because we were there, the student will necessarily turn to us. The trauma of the event may cause memories of these moments to be a blur or even to be completely repressed, and the student may not remember much of what we did. Above all, do not expect gratitude.

THE SCHOOL AS A COMMUNITY OF GRIEF

Some deaths affect the whole school community—an accident to a well-known member of the student body, the dramatic illness of a student, the death of a teacher or administrator, or the death of a prominent figure like President Kennedy. Other deaths may affect a smaller group in the school like a team, a club, or even a class. These occasions can be used for highly constructive ends. First, the feelings of the student body or class can be channeled into appropriate expressions of concern and ritual, so that students can resolve feelings that would otherwise remain upsetting for a long time or that would go into the subconscious. Second, students who have been members of a school community that handled death well will be able to cope with death in the various communities they will join as adults. Good teaching is not only a well-planned lesson but also good use of events that compel student interest.

There are rare times when a death occurs in or around school. For example, a first grader was killed by a car in front of the school in the presence of many students on their way into the building. In cases like this, once emergency measures have been seen to by police and mobile medical units, the facts surrounding the death should be made known by the administration to everyone in the school. Incomplete information together with imagination at times like these often leads to exaggerated versions of the death. An accurate account of the details of the incident allows the students and faculty to respond to the situation as it really exists.

When a member of the school community dies, appropriate responses should be arranged as soon as possible. The teacher can make sure that visitation times at the funeral home or at the family's home are well publicized, perhaps with a tactful lesson on funeral etiquette for the class. An address for personal sympathy notes can also be given. Groups of students might wish to plan more concrete expressions of concern. Perhaps some of the students will want to pay a condolence call with the teacher. It is traditional in many cultures that bereaved families do not prepare food for about a week, relying upon the community (other families and friends) to bring food. With families now often separated by long distances and the established traditions of the neighborhood disappearing, groups of students might want to arrange a schedule for making casseroles and cakes. There might be need for baby-sitting, transportation, or housecleaning that students could do. They might want to raise money for a memorial scholarship fund, medical research donations, or a cause especially commemorative of the dead person. In whatever they are able to do, students can find a way to channel the loss they feel into action. Then death will not leave them with a feeling of helplessness but will become an opportunity for human sharing.

Communal gathering is also important at the time of death. A death that is not recognized publicly is an unreal death. So it is appropriate that when the school community is diminished by one or more of its members, the loss be recognized. It can be recognized in an assembly in which there are simple eulogies or appropriate artistic presentations. The community can be given the chance to express its grief through literature about others who have grieved, by singing or listening to songs, or by shared silence. Smaller groups can share memories and thoughts about the deceased.

There may be some moral to be drawn from the life or death of the deceased, but moralizing is rarely useful. Few dead people are really as saintly as they may be painted, and students will be quick to catch hypocrisy. Drug overdoses or car accidents are dangers of the adolescent years, but students can draw their own conclusions without having adult admonitions hammered 'home. It will be easier for them to draw these conclusions if they have been allowed to feel and express their grief. Young children need reassurance that the death of one of their classmates from illness does not mean that they too can easily die at a young age. The comparative rarity of such deaths can be stressed.

After remembering and expressing loss, the school community needs to reconstitute itself, incorporating the loss and going on with the business of learning and living. If the loss has been a schoolwide one, a mourning period of a week might be observed with a display of photographs, art, poetry, or objects associated with the dead person. Such mourning periods allow a transition from the loss to normal functioning without making the grief seem just a brief interruption in everyday routine. The teacher needs to remember that the students may remain quiet and depressed for some time afterward (perhaps even a month) and that some students may begin to act out noisily and physically as a way of affirming that they are still alive. The class may displace anger and direct it toward the teacher because of frustrating and angry feelings they have about the loss. Such feelings are common and normal. The teacher can recognize angry feelings if they are present and encourage the students to focus on the loss and the deprivation that resulted. By accepting the anger the class may feel and suggesting action-oriented goals, the teacher can direct students to work off the energy that angry feelings engender (a car wash to raise money for a memorial donation, a dance, a basketball game, a gift of poems to send to the mourning family, activity of any kind that can be made meaningful). The sensitive teacher will be on the lookout for abnormal behavioral patterns that persist longer than ordinary periods of mourning (six months to a year to recover from a significant loss is not unusual). The teacher will not expect most students to be able to return to business immediately. Those who seem completely unaffected by what should have been a traumatic experience should also be closely observed in the ensuing months.

Death education becomes situation oriented when death crises occur at school, whether experienced by individual students or by the school community. In crisis situations, our willingness to be with our students develops models of behavior that can help them and influence them for many years to come.

FURTHER READING

GETSON, RUSSELL F., and DIXIE L. BENSHOFF, "Four Experiences of Death and How to Prepare to Meet Them," *School Counselor*, 24:5 (May 1977), 310–14.

JACKSON, EDGAR, *Telling a Child About Death*. New York: Channel Press, 1966.

JONES, WILLIAM H., "Death-Related Grief Counseling: The School Counselor's Responsibility," *School Counselor*, 24:5 (May 1977), 315–20.

KIRKPATRICK, J. and others, "Bereavement and School Adjustment," *Journal of School Psychology*, 3:4 (Summer 1965), 59–63.

KÜBLER–ROSS, Elisabeth, "The Languages of Dying," *Journal of Clinical Child Psychology*, 3:2 (Summer 1974), 22–24.

TEACHING
ABOUT
DEATH

Part **II**

The late medieval woodcuts of the dance of death show people from all stations in life—kings and monks, beggars and soldiers, and even teachers. Each of them has a skeleton as a partner in the dance. The motto engraved on those woodcuts is, "Remember O man that you shall die." The message seems to have been a comforting one, for the prints were very popular. People hung them in their cottages like soldiers hang pinups in their lockers. But it is not a message most of us want to hear, for we have grown up in a culture in which the reality of death is avoided physically and mentally. Yet the woodcut speaks truth, for we will die, and everyone we love will die or has

Personal Awareness of Death

Chapter **5**

already died. In interacting with young people about death, we are not encountering an unknown subject; we are dealing with something known all too well.

Our personal relationship with death has an effect on our roles as teacher and parent. Although the first part of this chapter is addressed more directly to professional educators, we recognize parents as the child's prime teachers. Although most of the early part of the chapter centers around the school setting, parents will be able to transfer insights from the classroom process to interactions with the child at home. School professionals are not alone in experiencing a dilemma in that person–profession relationship. One of the first problems confronting people who study the care of the dying has been how to overcome the personal reactions of medical personnel that interfere with their professional ability to render proper care. Sociologists—studying the hospital setting by standing in the halls and noting the frequency and duration of patients' visitation by hospital staff—reported that when a patient was diagnosed as terminal, there was an immediate drop both in time spent by the staff and in their frequency of contact in working with the patient. The status of the staff visiting the patient changed from heads of service or residents to interns, from registered nurses to licensed practical nurses. In one informal study, a supervising nurse asked a physician about the condition of a terminal patient. The physician reported that she was fine. The nurse asked if the physician had seen her. He said "no" but said that the floor nurse had reported to him. She asked the floor nurse if she had seen the patient and was told the report had come from an LPN. Further investigation showed that the LPN had received the report from an orderly who had talked to the only person to actually see the patient all day—the cleaning woman. Clearly, the discomfort the professionals felt in dealing with death was affecting their contact with the patient.

There are, however, values and attitudes that affect professional activities very positively. When we asked several nurses who we thought were excellent in working with dying people why they were able to do such a good job, almost all their replies began with good experiences with family or friends who had died. Their replies often started, "The good thing that came out of my mother's death. . . ." When they worked with dying people, it was their personal attitudes that made their work noticeably better. Experience has shown that when medical professionals are helped to examine their personal attitudes and responses to death, the quality of patient care improves immediately. As teachers and parents, we must do this same self-examination. In this chapter, we first talk about self-examination for teachers and counselors and then discuss the special place of self-examination in parenting.

PERSON AS PROFESSIONAL

In introducing death into the school curriculum, professionals are as much influenced, negatively and positively, by the attitudes and values they bring to the subject as are the medical professionals. One teacher—who as an adolescent had been revolted by the sight of his mother's embalmed body—could not relate to positive experiences his students had in a funeral home visit and so was not able to help them to integrate their learning experience. In every case of grieving with which a counselor came into contact, she repeated the only formula that had worked for her when her husband died: "We can't cry; we just have to go on living." She was unable to give the students the freedom to find their own pathways through mourning. On the other hand, a teacher whose brother had died when she was young was able to turn immediately to a poem in a school text that had helped her to express her emotions and that she now used in a fourth-grade class when they learned one of their class members had died in a car accident.

Death education, then, begins with the educator, for the first thing we bring to our children is ourselves. Sometimes the "look" of a certain child reminds us of a family member or a sweetheart or someone who is dead. How do we treat that child? Do we respond to good looks, extraordinary intellect, troubled souls, or flattery in nonprofessional ways? Are these ways in which our teaching provides an outlet for personal problems? If we had to wait until we were free from neurotic quirks before we started teaching, most of us would be unemployed.

We don't have to make ourselves psychological wizards in order to teach about death and dying. It is just necessary to recognize that personal life and professional life intersect in all our teaching about death. Because of the emotional impact of the subject of death and dying, we do a better and more professional job when we understand our interactions with it. Once we know what is going on inside ourselves, we will be able to understand better what is going on in the feelings and minds of our children. In the interface of personal life and professional life around death education, it is what we don't know that can hurt us. It is important to do a very careful self-examination of our past experiences and present relationship with death before teaching about it. This is true no matter how free we feel of problematic personal relations with death.

Some teachers feel that they can go right into a death curriculum because they have really begun teaching about death for very pragmatic reasons, such as wanting to look "up-to-date" because death education is popular right now or because students can be attracted into elective classes with the topic. But not everything that happens in school may be as simple as our reasons for beginning it. It is normal for significant personal material to be buried rather deeply. In thinking about death, past events and feelings affect us without our always being conscious of it. In a class for social work students, most of the people in the class are enrolled for the pragmatic reason that they expect that they will have to work with dying people someday and wish to be prepared for it. But in every class, a few students never seem able to complete the assignments or attend regularly. It becomes clear eventually that they are avoiding the class or assignments for personal reasons but are not aware of it. One student had forgotten about the dreams of death that had troubled her in early childhood. The course content made her uneasy, so she avoided those assignments that made her feel uncomfortable. When we helped her to recognize what was happening, she was able to function successfully in the course, though she would have failed otherwise. Teachers, too, can be lulled into a false sense of security about themselves when they think their initial agenda and motivation are not problematic. So though death education starts for practical reasons, we can be prepared for possible problems by giving some time to ourselves and our experiences with death.

Other teachers feel that they do not need this self-examination, because their reason for teaching is that they have some strong convictions about death and dying as it is experienced in the culture, and they think death education can be a way for them to focus on those convictions and help change the culture. We find that many teachers read books or view television shows on death in America and feel strongly that some aspects of current medical and funeral practices run counter to what they feel is right. Many have had experiences in hospitals or funeral homes that angered them or at the least, offended their sensibilities. These agenda are legitimate starting places for teaching and may even form a part of the class work at the junior and senior high school level. But if this is the reason for bringing death education to school, the teacher needs to be aware of the motivation and the emotions behind it. We must examine personal experiences that contributed to the formation of our ideas. Some of us have rather strong opinions about things that were never experienced directly. Others experience death and dying very directly, as when someone we love dies or when we come close to death ourselves, and these events and feelings remain indelibly imprinted on our minds. Was this experience shared by many others? Or were the circumstances of the death bizarre? or unusually tragic? or totally shocking? These experiences may cause our perspectives on other deaths and dying to be skewed or strongly prejudiced. By reviewing the experiences that were important in forming our values, we can achieve some distance on our opinions and be open to others who may have different experiences and consequently different values.

Strongly held opinions or ideological convictions often grow from deep within our psychological life. The campaigner against sex education who was quoted in the newspaper as saying, "Any girl who reads those books they are giving them would just want to go out and find a boy and have sex!" is probably saying more about herself than about the kids in school. So like the pragmatic agenda, the motivation behind our convictions ought to lead to an examination of our personal relationship with death.

Some of us know that we are bringing intense personal experiences with death to our professional role. Indeed, some of us have found death to be problematic in our lives and hope to make it less problematic for our students. Others have had losses in the past that we now feel we did not adequately work through at the time. Many have had periods of fear and anxiety centering around death. For some, the problematic areas are in the past; for others they are very much in the present.

Not all teachers of death education have the same emotional relationship with death. Some are more deeply affected by death than others, whether due to upbringing or the experience of many deaths with its consequent pain and loneliness. Some of us participate vicariously in the books we read or the movies we see, but somehow our lives have not been touched directly by loss. The lucky ones are fortunate only in not yet having had to come to that pain of loss and separation that everyone must inevitably face, for death is the ultimate, unavoidable experience. Each of us, whether we admit it or not, is dancing with the skeleton in the woodcut, and in teaching about death, our own dance of death will affect our performance in the classroom.

How do we prepare personally for teaching about death in school? Those who have suffered deep pain must look at the pain again to check that there is nothing hidden that will affect their teaching. Those who have not yet known that pain closely need to know what it feels like, for the study of death—both for students and ourselves— cannot uncover feelings and thoughts previously repressed or unknown. The rest of this chapter is a personal preparation for our professional roles, whether we fall into the first category or the second.

REMEMBERING THE PAST

There are many ways to recover our past experiences with death. What means we use depends on personal style and the intensity of past experience. Here are some ways other teachers have found helpful:

"I asked my mother to tell me how I reacted when I was eight years old and my uncle and grandfather died within two weeks of each other."

"A group I belonged to helped me by sharing their memories. It was amazing how many were like mine, only I had forgotten them."

"The death that was most significant to me was my dad's. I got out the photographs of him and spent an evening reliving those weeks just before and after his death. I found some things were still bothering me that I hadn't realized before."

"My wife had brain surgery a couple of years ago, and it was touch and go for a while. One night I was thinking about that time—so I started talking into a tape recorder. A couple of days later, I listened to the tape. A lot of things about what I was afraid of became very clear, and I have been able to think about them a lot lately."

"I took a course in death and dying at the college to learn what I needed to teach. One of the assignments was to write about our own experiences with death. It was good for me to learn where my sore spots were, but I also learned when I listened to what others said."

One of the most interesting things about our past experiences with death as they affect the present is that reality and psychic reality are the same. That is, we can be just as affected in the present by childhood fears and dreams about death as by real deaths. In the same way, the line between fantasy and memory becomes blurred when remembering our past and death. When has death touched our lives? Let us examine the memories one by one. Those from childhood may be at the same time deeply etched and recoverable and yet clouded by childhood misunderstandings and perception. It is not unusual for adults to remember the death of a pet as being more important to them than the death of a grandparent or other family member. Taking out each memory, we need to try separating fact from fantasy. Both fact and fantasy are important, for we respond to both, but our responses can be more clearly seen if we retrospectively separate them. How did we feel at the time? Not all our feelings are appropriate. Many people find that they responded with curiosity instead of sadness, wondering what was going on. One of our own children, on learning of his grandfather's death, was glad, because that meant that his uncle from California would be coming to visit. Very often children feel anger or fright at being excluded from the rest of the grieving family. Sometimes our response was not to the death but to how those around us acted. Was Mamma not paying attention to us because we had been bad? If a significant death occurred in our mid-teen years, it is very common for us to remember most clearly that we did not cry or respond as we would have wished. These inappropriate emotions often carry with them feelings of guilt or shame that we did not grieve or respond spontaneously because we really did not love the dead as much as we thought we should. Mixed with our response is the guilt or shame not only at how we acted but also at how we felt.

> Phyllis, a graduate student, was bothered by the death of a friend when they were both ten, and she remembered going to all the rooms in the school asking for blood donations for the friend she loved. As she talked about the memory, she realized that she had made that request only in her own classroom and then remembered that she resented having to play with the girl who had died because she really didn't like her. When she was able to finish the difficult job of getting the memory straight, a task that also involved talking to her mother and the dead girl's mother, Phyllis was able to recognize the source of troublesome feelings she was having. She had been remembering the friend as someone she loved, but the buried feelings were based on the real situation of being forced to play with someone she didn't like. Once she understood the conflict and guilt of her childhood feelings, she was able to understand her uncomfortable response when coping with death in the present.

If there is trouble separating event from fantasy or if events elude us the more we try to think about them, we probably need some help. The best resources may be those who lived through the death with us, that is, family or friends who also remember. They have gone through the same trauma, so we have to be alert to the fact that their remembrance may be just as much mixed with fantasy as our own. If they were adults when the death occurred (and we were not), we can ask them what they perceived as happening at the time of death. It would not be unusual to discover that we were lied to or excluded at that time. One man felt guilty for not being present at his beloved grandfather's bedside when he died because he was playing baseball. Five years later, he learned that it was planned that he not be there, because life supports had been turned off. He had overheard the lie told his grandmother that the death was unexpected and had believed that lie in the ensuing years. He had to deal with present feelings of anger over the lie he was told and rid himself of familiar and uncomfortable guilt. Some people have been able to locate family records that tell the story. Such records (most often letters) are more likely to be saved than others, so it is worthwhile to look for them. If we still have trouble separating event from imagination, then perhaps a friend or counselor will be available who will listen. Many people find that as they speak, things become clearer than when they conduct an internal dialogue.

For some of us, one of the memories we need to remove is that of almost dying ourselves. The memory is usually quite clear, though not always. We need to remember our first reactions to the possibility of our death and then subsequent thoughts about dying. It is not uncommon for people in great pain to want to die in order not to feel the pain. Many others find that it is not death they are afraid of, but leaving those they love or facing interminable suffering. As with the deaths of others, there is still a need to separate fact from imagination.

Having verified as much as we can about our involvement with death and dying situations, we must now try to relive the painful experiences. Some of our reliving will serve to remind us of what our students may be going through now or help to make theories personally under-standable, so that our teaching and counseling becomes more dynamic. Reexperiencing painful memories may have a therapeutic value. There may be strong feelings many years later attached to memories of death. Many times there is "unfinished business" (guilt, anger, feelings of abandonment, and so on) hanging over the memory. It is a good idea to resolve such problems before taking up death education, for those feelings and "unfinished business" are exactly what will cause blind spots in our per-ception of what students are experiencing. Those feelings may blind us to what students need in lesson plans, to what material will be most meaningful, and to what issues should be appropriately considered in the school setting.

The mechanism through which old feelings and un-finished business cause blind spots is very simple, but in its simplicity, it is also very deceptive. We all function in ways that tend to avoid discomfort. We move into situa-tions that allow us to function comfortably in order to avoid pain and stress wherever possible. The feelings at-tached to traumatic memories may cause perceptible or suppressed feelings of discomfort in various aspects of death and dying situations, and therefore we may avoid that discomfort without being conscious of doing it. That avoidance can be a blind spot. There are two ways to over-come this comfort–discomfort mechanism. First, we can work through the feelings and "finish the business." Sec-ond, we can recognize where we still hurt and be prepared for discomfort when it returns. Most people use a combi-nation of both ways in preparing for death education and counseling in school.

Reliving the old experiences can cause pain again, but it is worth it if the pain can give way to joyous memories or recovered memory. Indeed, regaining the past as fully as possible can help us to have a fuller present. We can trust ourselves to let the memory and its pain come in our reexperiencing. If the death was a difficult one and we suspect that the memory would be difficult to handle alone, we can ask someone trustworthy to be with us. Like our students confronting death, when we know someone is in control, we can give ourselves permission to be out of control. We must try not to avoid painful memories as they appear. In separating fact from fantasy, we may find that the pain is different than the remembered pain at the time of the death. If the feelings are powerful, we can allow them to come out and be fully expressed, knowing that by going through the feelings, we can resolve them—get rid of them forever! Sometimes a good cry can clean out a lot of painful garbage; sometimes telling the dead that we are angry with them for leaving or that we feel unloved because they abandoned us can allow us to get to the better feelings that are on the other side of negative emotions.

For many people, the kinds of examination and reexperiencing just outlined will be enough. But a few others will find that once they have discovered the loaded memories in their minds, they will feel the need to come to terms with those memories in a more direct way. Usually it is unfinished business that seems to compel exposure of the memory rather than its suppression. Our advice here is: Go with the feeling. The human mind is conditioned to accept loss. Paths seem to be built into the psyche that will lead to resolutions. We can recognize those paths by our feelings. Often the feeling is one of needing to communicate directly with someone who died long ago.

We must be careful here, for often feelings of wanting

to communicate with the dead grow from an inability to lead lives independent of those who have died. Sometimes there is a wish to recapture the secure feeling of being taken care of that was paramount in that relationship. Except in a metaphoric sense, this longing for security with the dead cannot be fulfilled. We remember well meeting with an eighty-two-year-old widow who, as the conversation progressed, said, "Now I want you to meet Roger," and then took out a picture of her husband, deceased for more than twenty-five years. He had been a school principal, remembered as an important person by many people in town. His widow was one of the most active and caring people we have ever known, and when asked how she always seemed to know just the right thing to say or do, she said, "I just do what I think Roger would do." The dead do continue to influence our lives in this way, but beyond this metaphoric sense, it is impossible to live depending on a relationship that is now over.

But some of us feel the need to say good-bye to the dead—that there are words still to be said and feelings to be expressed. Many people experience the feeling of the presence of a deceased loved one that seems to be comforting for those who are older and at times, frightening for those who are younger. When some kind of contact with the dead occurs, it is often a way to communicate something important and gain insight.

> Joan, a graduate student, realized during a course on death that she was still upset by the death of her mother when she was fourteen. One evening while taking a shower, she saw her mother's face on the shower wall and started talking to her. She told her how angry she was for having to spend those important high school years without a mother. Joan yelled and screamed, but after the anger was expressed, she could then tell her mother

how much she missed her. She stood in the shower crying as she told her mother about high school events and then about her college years, about her successes and failures, about significant people she now knew. And finally she was able to tell her mother that she had never told her how much she loved her. And then it was over. The next week when she came to the office to tell about it, before she started the story, we observed aloud that there was something different, something calmer and happier about her.

A technique some people find helpful

There is a technique for those who feel that they have unfinished business with the dead but who do not have a feeling of being able to be in contact: Find a comfortable place where you will be insured a few hours of privacy, and put an empty chair opposite you, mentally placing the person in the chair. Sometimes a photograph or special memento in the chair helps to picture the person sitting there. Even if you feel a little silly at first, you will find that the person opposite will become more real as you tell what is in your heart. Speaking as if the person were there, say what you have always wanted to say but never had the chance. At the outset, it is easier if you have some idea of what you want to say or what events you want to talk about. It is important to express negative as well as positive things if the negative things are there. Some people find it helpful to change chairs and answer as if they were the dead person. Others don't want to do this. Just follow your feelings here. In the dialogue with the dead person, you might be surprised where feelings will lead. You might have to forgive or be forgiven. You might also have to say, "You bastard, I can live without you."

Whatever happens is what will happen, but in risking the experience, we can trust that the human psyche is able to deal with grief and that there is nothing in our relationship with the dead that can hurt once it is in the open. Usually the end of this experience is spent in quiet, peaceful remembering. Most people who use this technique find that talking about it with a competent counselor for a few sessions helps to put the material that emerged into healing perspective. One teacher who used this technique successfully was able to think about and recall memories of her father whose unusual and shocking death twelve years before had closed her off to all feelings and thoughts about him since then. Saying good-bye and telling him of her life over those last years restored the meaning of her father's life to her present experience.

OLD FEARS AND FANTASIES

There is more in our past concerning death than the events we can reexperience. Tied to those events are imagined events that in turn become the basis for some very strong feelings in the present. There are also past fears and images that were not attached to events connected to real deaths. All of us participated in some way in fears expressed in childhood superstitions and cultural and religious beliefs.

Did you ever see a hearse go by
Remember you may be next to die.

They wrap you up in a big white sheet
And put you down about six feet deep.
The worms crawl in and the worms crawl out,
The worms play pinochle in your snout.
And then you turn an icky green,
And your guts come out like whipping cream.

A class of adults, upon hearing this familiar children's chant, responded with uneasy and embarrassed laughter as their childhood fears were remembered and relived.

Freud discovered that imagined events in the past could have just as much effect on the present as real trauma. He called this psychic reality. For our purposes, all we need to understand about old fears and fantasies is that they can affect our present lives only when they remain unconscious. In a few cases, fears and fantasies are symbolic of deeper problems. That is, death fears may indicate psychological problems, but unless other symptoms exist (and unless we have been urged by others to seek therapy), we can assume that just recognizing fears and fantasied events is enough. The key to understanding is that when our fears remain unspoken and largely out of our consciousness, they can hurt our professional performance by making us uncomfortable. As soon as we know why we feel uncomfortable, we can act in ways that do not allow this material to interfere with our professional lives.

To do this, the fantasy material is made conscious; we need to expose it to the light of our reasoning minds. Being conscious of it does not mean the imaginary material is discarded or downgraded; some of this material will lead to profound insights into ourselves and the nature of being human. There are many ways to do this kind of "consciousness" raising. Writing can be very helpful. In every college class on death and dying we teach, a number of students find that keeping a journal or diary of their memories is a meaningful assignment. Since the older material is often deeply buried, poetry seems a natural way for some to express it, whereas others use prose. The idea of writing is not to produce publishable works but to get it out where our eyes and minds can come to terms with it. Talking is another useful means, though talking to ourselves is not usually helpful. We can ask someone to listen and ask questions when he does not understand. This helps us to clarify what is in our own minds. A tape recorder can be a good listening ear if we speak into it as if we were trying to make the memory clear to someone else. It is a good idea to wait about a day before listening to the tape, so we can hear ourselves more objectively. All the ways we suggested previously for finding memories of events also work for fantasy, including talking to those from our past who were around at the time the fantasy was produced.

There may be some events that we are not sure really happened, but they seem too real to be imagined. This is normal, because some fantasy is so powerful in the area of death that it seems to move to a different level of consciousness. It is very common for people describing dreams about death, especially dreams of those who have died recently, to say, "It was not like other dreams, it seemed more real." It is also normal because there are events connected with death that fall outside commonly accepted social reality in Western culture. There has been publicity about the strange experiences many people report when they are observed to be clinically dead and then are resuscitated. These people are coming forward now because the culture is changing to a point where such experiences are not necessarily labeled as psychotic or abnormal. Almost half the population responds affirmatively to a survey question about being in contact with those who have died. In our research with grieving and dying people, we have found that the fear of being insane is very often connected to postdeath contact and out-of-body experiences. That is, people do not realize that the experiences are normal and so assume that they are "going crazy"—or hallucinating. The experiences are very normal. They are part of the way we deal with death. They may even point to realms of experience not usually available to us—Wordsworth called them "intimations of immortality"—though what we believe about these experiences, other than their reality to us, is a matter of faith and not science. When we cannot be sure if an experience is real or imagined, it is not helpful to spend much time trying to decide which it is. We can ask, "What does it mean to us now?" and "What did it mean to us when it happened?" and pursue this line of investigation instead of trying to make a distinction between psychic reality and experiential reality.

When these memories of events—real and imagined—are recalled, we cannot sterilize them. They may still be mysterious, frightening, and even tragic, as they were before. Indeed, if we succeed in trivializing memory, we would be doing the greatest possible disservice to ourselves and our children, for we would be making death into nothing, and if death is nothing, life itself becomes valueless. Death limits all human experience, and life becomes meaningful only when we learn to live within that limitation. For many people, death means loneliness and abandonment. Yet it is only as we realize our loneliness that we can appreciate closeness with and commitment to another person. For many people, death is frightening because time is running out, but only when we realize that time is not limitless can we begin to cherish our days and hours. Death can be feared because it is unknown, but recognizing that unknown allows us to live in a world full of other mysteries that give life a far richer texture than when everything is seen in the clear light of rational thinking. To understand, in even a limited way, the meaning of death is to understand life at its most profound. If the tragic, sad, or frightening feelings that are gathered around memories, dreams, and fantasies about death are taken away, we have only succeeded in making life less meaningful. Humans are the only animals, so far as we know, who can reflect on their own mortality. Suppressing the feelings associated with that reflection takes away our humanness.

We said earlier in this chapter that it is not necessary to be psychological wizards in order to teach about death and dying. What we do have to do is try to know ourselves. In this task of self-examination, we become more psychologically healthy. After all, what is mental health but the ability to perceive and respond appropriately to the world as it really is in the present? Death is part of that real world, and we are healthy when our perceptions and responses are based on that reality. Many of us have grown up in a culture where death has not been recognized as the ultimate reality. That denial makes American culture neurotic about death and dying, and if we find in our personal experience of death that we do not share cultural norms, that social rituals surrounding death seem flat and plastic, then we may be the ones who have become mentally healthier. If anything, death shows us that we are human and only human, that we live in a world where death is a reality but that we share the world with others with whom, for some brief moments, there is love, happiness, and caring. Life at times may be something to cry about. In knowing and feeling these possibilities of life experience, we are then ready to teach about death.

BEING CAUGHT OFF GUARD

Even after intensive self-preparation, it is still possible for problems we had not foreseen to come up in our work. What follows is a look forward to some of the kinds of problems that can arise as we teach and counsel about death in school. Fortunately, with careful preparation we can be reasonably sure that we will not be caught off guard too often.

The first problem that may come up is the emergence of personal material not yet examined as we did self-preparation. One teacher thought her grandfather's death had not been problematic for her but found, when a junior high school class was debating prolongation of life by machines, that she had very strong feelings that she then connected to the last six weeks of her grandfather's dying. It is difficult, of course, to see that there might be some sort of a problem that is intruding into our professional lives. The real mark of the experienced death educator is that he or she is in touch with personal responses all the time. Once we realize that some unexamined history or emotion is intruding into our work, that intellectual awareness enables us to control it. All of which is to say that once the problem is identified, we are on the way to solving it. The procedure is the same self-examination suggested earlier, though it may be a good idea to use the therapeutic professionals to help speed the process if it is interfering badly with our work at school.

The question raised, however, is a moot one: "How do we know when our personal history is interfering with our professional activity?" It would be nice if there were easy answers to the question. If, after some very honest self-examination, the answer to any of the following questions is "no," we may have a problem or area of further investigation:

> —Am I able to hear what my students are saying to me the first time, so they do not find it necessary to try to say it again, or do they turn away from my answer and talk no more about it?
>
> —Do I find that I look forward positively to the sessions dealing with death and dying?
>
> —Are there areas that I avoid talking about in counseling situations or as part of a death and dying curriculum?
>
> —Am I afraid of expressing emotion in the classroom or in counseling or of having my students become emotional?

Unfortunately, failure in death education is too often an indicator that our personal and professional lives are not integrated. To be sure, there may be many reasons for a single session or even a whole unit to go badly. Failure cries out for analysis, for there is a reason somewhere. In death education, the reason is often that our personal and professional lives did not mesh properly.

Another problem that may emerge is our response to encounters with death that come for the first time as part of the teaching experience.

> Marjorie, a sixth-grade teacher, had never really thought about dead bodies. While touring a funeral home in preparation for her

class's visit, the mortician showed her the embalming room with a corpse in it. She vaguely recalled seeing the embalmed body of her grandmother at her funeral, but she found that this rather stark encounter with a corpse set off many feelings she didn't know she had. The children, of course, would not have been shown the room with a corpse present, but in her preparation, Marjorie found that she was confronted with unexpected negative feelings. With this experience behind her but without adequate dealing with the aroused feelings, this teacher had a very difficult time with the death curriculum she was teaching, especially with the trip to the funeral home that took place a few days after her preparatory visit.

Myron, a third-grade teacher, found that he was becoming sad as he read the stories he was selecting to read to his class. *A Time for Blackberries* brought tears each time he read it. Yet he could not account for this sadness in his feelings from the past. No one he loved had died, nor could he remember any deaths of his peers. Though he had never deeply grieved before, Myron was now experiencing grief as he worked with the material.

His situation was not different from that of the students, many of whom are presented with the idea of death for the first time in school. When this happens to teachers and counselors, there is more pressure, because we know our personal response affects our work, and we cannot quietly withdraw during the class period as a student can. A careful study of materials beforehand can help alleviate the problem of being caught off guard emotionally.

A third kind of problem that can come up is our response to the student's reaction to death.

Jane had never been in contact with grieving people in a problematic way but found that she was responding negatively to the weepy, withdrawn way one student acted after she read a short story about the death of a parent. Jane knew that both the child's parents were living and even called home to make sure her information was correct. She found herself getting very angry with the child and feeling that the child was "stupid and uncontrolled" to act that way. When she talked about it with her mother, she was reminded that those were the same words she had used of a cousin she didn't like when, the year before, the cousin had broken off a love affair.

Weepy and withdrawn behavior seemed to make this teacher uncomfortable, possibly because it was unacceptable behavior for herself and she defended against exhibiting it or possibly because it was associated with situations and/or persons she disliked. Another teacher was able to accept most of the responses to the subject as OK but was annoyed by those children who used laughter and jokes as a way of expressing their nervousness about the subject. We may be alert to personal reactions to the subject, but it would be impossible to foresee every circumstance and our reaction to it, so we might as well trust ourselves and deal with the situations as they arise.

When the teacher who thought the child was "stupid and uncontrolled" realized that she was responding to her estimation of her cousin and not the student, she could refocus and respond to the child. When the teacher "practiced" grieving by reading *A Time for Blackberries*, he was able to realize that he was but one griever among many in the room, and when children cried over the story, he could understand their sentiment all the more. The teacher who encountered the corpse reported that she went on with the lesson plans, but "I just really watched myself whenever we came to anything that had to do with bodies." Professional therapeutic counseling may be indicated whenever we feel out of control in our responses.

A special note to those who have recently experienced a significant death or who may be facing one in the near future.

Perhaps you should consider not teaching or counseling directly with death and dying issues right now. The experience of your loss leaves you understandably in a vulnerable and sapped condition. You need time to recover and reconstruct your life. It is not fair to ask yourself to be constantly reopening painful wounds that heal slowly with time, but that is what you would be doing if you dealt with death and dying now. It is true that as someone who is participating in the dying and grieving process, you will be more sensitive to what is going on within you and around you, and this awareness will enhance your ability to work effectively in death education. There is no reason to force yourself into now painful areas. It is not a cop-out to decide to give yourself some time to recover.

If you do decide to go ahead and teach about death and dying while you are in the middle of some death-related crisis, trust yourself, but don't try to hide from yourself or others what is going on in your life. It is especially important not to try to fool students by pretending that you are not involved in the subject when in fact you are. They will be able to sense that something is going on, and sensing that will make them uncomfortable. You might also want to know where a trusted listener is available and check yourself out from time to time to see that you are not overtaxing yourself emotionally as you try to cope with person and profession under difficult circumstances.

PARENTING
AND DEATH

As parents, we bring to our relationship with our children the same problems in our personal background as do teachers. It is important then to do the same rigorous self-examination, for it is in their relationship with us that our children form most of their basic attitudes toward death. Whereas the teacher is confronted with students mostly in groups and with a formal agenda for the day, interaction with our children is far more informal, with questions or comments about death likely to come rather spontaneously. Our reactions to comments and questions are as important as what we say in more composed moments, for our children are far more in tune to the subtleties of our emotions than they can be to the teacher's. Though the child may not be able to articulate it intellectually, the meaning of our pauses, nervous quickness, downcast glances, or tear-filled eyes is understood emotionally and internalized by the child. With our children, very often we communicate not to "do what I do" or "do what I say" but to "be what I am." This is, of course, a rather frightening thought to some of us, for there is often the hope that our offspring will have an easier time with life's problems than we do. But again, we do not have to make ourselves into psychological wizards in order to offer our children a healthier world view about death than perhaps we had.

Our past experiences with death will interfere with effective parenting only when we are not aware of how that past is affecting the present. Upon articulation of our attitudes about death, our children can objectify and acquire some distance from them, so as to be able to handle what we say intellectually before internalizing it. The honest statement, "I'm uncomfortable with that question because I had a very hard time when my father died," allows the child to put our response in perspective. Though such perspective can be seen only to a limited extent by younger children, it can be seen by those in the intermediate grades as they begin to form identities that are separate from their relationship with us. By the junior high school years, children are already looking rather objectively at their parents (indeed, it may seem to us that they are too objective). But honest statements about our past will allow the teenagers to accept us as we are and then allow them to find their own response to the meaning of death within the family.

It would be too bad, however, if we got the idea that we, as the elder generation, have nothing to offer. We have received some insights and ways of responding to death that young people need and are at times anxious to have. To be sure, our answers are often not as clear as we would like them to be. So the honest answer of, "When my father died, my grandmother said to me. . . ." is a helpful answer, even if it is followed by the equally honest, "Sometimes I find it hard to really believe that, but it still seems true." A recounting of the findings of our self-examination can also be very helpful to children. One mother responded to a seven-year-old's comment on God, not liking someone so they die, by saying: "When I was a little girl and my dog died, I thought for a long time that it was because I had been bad. But later I knew the dog was just old and sick, and I had been too young to understand that." She had not remembered those early thoughts until she had taken a course on death at the community college and had been asked to write her memories. Another mother told a five-year-old that as a child, she too had thought a monster was coming in the bedroom to kill her and she had had to use a night-light. Then she and the child shared how nice night-lights were. In reporting this to us, she said she had not remembered about the monster until a year earlier, when she was a member of a group examining their past encounters with death.

There is one time when our response to death is of special importance in the way we deal with children. That is when we and our child are responding to the same death. Unlike teachers, parents cannot postpone interacting with children when they are experiencing a special loss in their lives or when they are facing their own deaths. At that time, parents cannot expect to be able to put their responses in a neat, intelligible package for their children, for the ambivalences and wide-ranging thoughts and emotions that accompany any death are too strong to be nicely wrapped up for the child. Nor can parents expect themselves to put their feelings aside for a neutral moment in which they explain what is happening to the child. Rather, as parents we need to share grief with our children. What the child feels is not what we feel, for the loss will be a different one—we lose a spouse, the child a parent; we lose a parent, the child a grandparent—and the child will respond at his or her level of development. But if we have examined our past relationship with death, we will know what we are experiencing and be able to monitor ourselves in two important ways. First, we can make sure that in our grief we do not alienate ourselves from our child. That is, we can share the grief with the child so that he or she understands why we are acting as we are and that it is not because of something the child has thought or done. Behavior that has an explanation will not mystify the child and cause problems in the future. Second, we can attempt to separate our response to death from the child's response, allowing the child to express what he or she is really feeling and not what the child thinks we want felt or said.

Later, when the immediate pain of death is over, we can talk to our children about what they and we have been through and how we were and are now affected by the death. This sharing is a continuation of the process of understanding ourselves in our experience with death. As we share with our children, we start them on the process of self-reflection.

FURTHER READING

GORDON, DAVID COLE, *Overcoming the Fear of Death*. New York: Macmillan, 1970.

KALISH, RICHARD, and DAVID REYNOLDS, *Death and Ethnicity: A Psychocultural Study*. Los Angeles, Calif.: University of Southern California Press, 1976.

KASTENBAUM, ROBERT, *Death, Society, and Human Experience*. St. Louis, Mo.: C. V. Mosby, 1977.

————, and RUTH AISENBERG, *The Psychology of Death*. New York: Springer, 1972.

KOESTENBAUM, PETER, *Is There an Answer to Death?* Englewood Cliffs, N.J.: Prentice-Hall, 1976.

KÜBLER-ROSS, ELISABETH, *On Death and Dying*. New York: Macmillan, 1969.

MOODY, RAYMOND A., *Life After Life.* Atlanta, Georgia: Mockingbird Books, 1975.

NEALE, ROBERT E., *The Art of Dying.* New York: Harper & Row, 1973.

PATTISON, E. MANSELL, ed., *The Experience of Dying.* Englewood Cliffs, N.J.: Prentice-Hall, 1977.

SHEPARD, MARTIN, *Someone You Love Is Dying.* New York: Harmony Books, 1975.

SUDNOW, DAVID, *Passing On.* Englewood Cliffs, N.J.: Prentice-Hall, 1967.

What kinds of goals do we have for the children in our care? We would like our children to be knowledgeable about death and the process of dying; we would like them to have the personal and emotional resources to cope with death in a healthy way; we would like them to make informed decisions about medical and funeral choices; and we would like them to be socially and ethically aware of issues relating to death and dying.

There are different dimensions of death education. One kind of death education takes place within the family context, and the other in the structured context of the school setting. Yet basically, the goals remain the same.

Goals in Death Education

Chapter **6**

One dimension exists when the school socializes the child within the general culture, another when the family transmits its particular values, attitudes, and traditions. There is a different emotional quality to the relationships formed at school as compared to those at home. There is the difference between the formal learning process of the school and the informal learning process that occurs within the family. It is easier to conceptualize formal goals in the structured setting before discussing the realization of these goals at home. Parents and school professionals will be able understand what is involved in death education more concretely if we begin with the school.

The goals we choose for class are our answer to the question of what we want our students to get out of death education. Our answers can be couched in terms of behavioral objectives defining both the overall program and the individual parts of the units, or the answers may be couched in more general terms to which each unit points. No matter how formally we state our goals, death education presents some special challenges, because the newness of the subject provides no past references. We must therefore find goals from our own experience. Further, most school systems do not yet have systematic programs in death education that provide an organizing schema for each grade or teacher. Teachers who introduce death education into their classrooms now do so because of some need the teachers themselves perceive. This means that we must be rather rigorous in defining our thinking, so goals are not amorphous. By establishing goals, the process of planning activities and gathering resources becomes easier, for we have a standard by which to judge ideas and materials. If we know our goals, it will be easy to evaluate our teaching, because all we have to do is find out if we have accomplished what we set out to do.

The current state of death education calls for a good deal of creativity, for there are few good "cookbook" packages we can buy. This means that the teachers who are the most successful are those who have a genuine interest in what they are doing. There are four general goals that emerge as centers around which it is possible to structure death education:

1. to inform the students of facts not currently widespread in the culture;
2. to make the student an informed consumer of medical and funeral services;
3. to make the student an informed consumer of medical and funeral services;
4. to help the student formulate socioethical issues related to death and define value judgments these issues raise.

After choosing one or more of these, the teacher will then delineate more concrete goals for a particular class and situation. The curriculum material listed in Chapter 7 should help teachers move from the general goal to the specific age-appropriate activity.

Clearly these general goals are interrelated, for the material that is covered in one goal may also be a necessary part of another. For example, we cannot expect students to make consumer decisions if they do not know some basic facts about death. In the same way, we find that as students are given a chance to examine their response to the idea of their own death and the death of significant others, they are better equipped to examine socioethical issues. But the general goals as goals are distinct, for they are ways we as teachers can focus what we are trying to do in the classroom.

We have outlined each goal that follows in terms of the questions raised, a sampling of ways to accomplish the goal, a brief sketch of the material included within the goal, and guidelines for evaluation.

GOAL ONE: To inform the student about facts not currently widespread in the culture.

This goal provides answers to the question, "What happens when people die?" Death has been a taboo topic for discussion until recently. This means there has been widespread ignorance of such elementary facts as legal and medical definitions of death, the effect of advancing medical technology upon the life span, common hospital practices concerning the dying and their families, the nature and cost of funeral industry services, appropriate social and religious rituals at the time of death, and ways of coping with death in other times and in other cultures. Due to the previous reluctance of society to sanction such discussions, we might say that everyone needs a generalized remedial education. Folklore provides the background for much knowledge about death and dying. Questions that students naturally ask are worth exploring, because they ultimately point to the students' curiosity and fears about their own deaths and those of loved ones. The reason we have been unable to educate our children is because of our own fears and ignorance about death. Students can initiate their study with a basic biological definition of life and death adapted to the level of the students' understanding. There are now differing definitions of death, and several states are in the process of rewriting statutes defining these criteria. Since the legal definitions are based on medical practices, these statutes form a core for discussion of what death is at junior and senior high school levels.

In the earliest grades, any project involving birth and growth can be expanded to include death. "How does the seed become a flower?" and "What happens to the plant if it doesn't have enough sun, soil, or water?" are really questions along the same continuum of inquiry. Children find dead birds all the time and bring them to the classroom. The nature of death can be established in a short discussion of "What's wrong with it?" "What might have happened to it?" and "Can we make it well?" The death of classroom pets and plants can be used in the same way. If we bury the animal or plant, the children can develop some basic knowledge of decomposition and the nitrogen cycle as well as of funeral procedure.

The next important area of study is the dynamics of family grief, that is, the way people respond and cope after facing traumatic loss. Students need to know how people behave when they grieve and in what ways our society provides means to express natural and healing displays of grief. This will help them understand those around them as well as the meaning of pain and loss when they look seriously at their own grief.

Death is a social event within the family and community, so it is important to consider the effect of death on the social and religious circles surrounding an individual and the ways various societies respond to death. Social and religious rituals concerning funeral practices and the mourning period can be investigated historically and cross-culturally. The teacher may explore these effectively through examination of different practices of the various ethnic groups in the classroom or by linking the study of death to anthropologically based studies.

In the study of death customs in their own culture, students can role play the various roles of family, friends, pallbearers, clergy, funeral director, and so forth. They can have a discussion of the etiquette, responsibilities, and possible feelings of each one. One of the ways of leading into a discussion on local funeral customs is to ask the students to bring in obituaries from the daily newspaper. Careful reading of the obituary notices will show the students what different religious customs are practiced. The students may also write their own epitaphs or compose eulogies for each other, perhaps after a study of famous epitaphs and eulogies.

Evaluation

If this goal has been achieved, the students should be able to demonstrate their mastery of essential factual material at their grade level. They should be able to show familiarity with the basic biological and psychological processes surrounding death and the social institutions interacting with these processes.

GOAL TWO: To help the student affectively deal with the idea of personal death and the deaths of significant others.

This goal helps the student find ways to answer the question, "How can I cope with the reality of death in my life in a healthy way?" The taboo against discussing death with others results in a climate of isolation and avoidance when death troubles us. When we cannot share our experiences and have others share theirs with us, we cannot know whether what we feel is acceptable and real. Feelings and thoughts that stay in our own heads only go around in circles, never going anywhere new—they don't move to resolution or acceptance.

We must remember that we can never totally take away the fear of the student's own death, for that fear is realistic—we will all die someday. We also cannot completely take away the pain of deaths the students have experienced. There is no way the scar left in a child's life by the premature death of a parent can be erased, but the death can be accepted. We can mourn together and comfort each other for the deaths we have known. In doing so, we create a community of mourning that is healing and far preferable to solitary grief.

The experience, then, is one of sharing feelings and thoughts. The teacher becomes a facilitator for this sharing by the careful selection of poetry, literature, and visual media that will call forth emotions associated with loss and separation. Students can express their feelings and perceptions about death situations with each other in class and will discover their common experience as well as their ability to help each other by listening.

At times the classroom becomes a community of grief, such as at the death of a student or someone close to a student. Few children of school age are completely untouched by death experiences in their own lives. Young children suffer losses—even if it is a turtle or fish, or a friend who is moving—more than adults realize. The classroom then becomes the setting for shared feelings of empathy and fear and for questions that arise as a natural consequence of the anxiety experienced by the children.

There has been a flurry of publicity about the extraordinary, psychic, or ecstatic experiences that often accompany death. After children are old enough to separate fantasy from reality (usually after age ten), these experiences may be presented as further ways people accept death. It is meaningful to introduce older students to these experiences, which often accompany dying and grieving. The fact that these experiences may be considered abnormal or linked with the occult in our culture leads people to deny them as a means of reintegrating their lives after a loss. Simply presenting the material gives students permission to use these phenomena as a healing force in their own lives. Children's beliefs and fantasies about death and what happens after death can also be explored. The teacher need not worry about raising general religious ideas such as resurrection, heaven, afterlife, and so on, since all religions have something to say about these concepts, and a free exchange of ideas should only confirm the commonality of shared human experience. Perhaps the students can check with their families as to what they believe and share that in class. We do not believe that the teacher should provide his or her own religious beliefs on these matters. It is the function of the teacher to initiate and guide the discussion, not to use it for proselytizing.

Evaluation

It is very difficult to evaluate affective learning, for its acquisition will only be in evidence when death and grieving affect the child directly. Yet the teacher can have some sense as to whether the goal has been achieved in the comfort levels students demonstrate in their interactions with those who have experienced a loss and in the fullness with which they allow themselves to mourn personal losses. The teacher can also informally evaluate the learning by the awareness level of the students about their own feelings and the resources they are able to bring to bear in handling their fears.

GOAL THREE: To make the student an informed consumer of medical and funeral services.

People rarely die at home today. Most people die in institutions surrounded by life-sustaining medical equipment. Our individuality is often lost within the institutional framework. In order to combat this problem, students can learn to be responsible for family and personal care by exercising their legal rights within health-care systems, such as those outlined in the Patient's Bill of Rights (see appendix). Modern medical technology allows the physician to make decisions about expensive and painful procedures that the patient and family may not wish to have. Physicians today seem to be more willing to have the patient and family share these decisions. If the family and patient decline to exercise their responsibility, fear of malpractice suits and his/her own sense of medical ethics will often force the physician to take measures he or she would not want personally in a similar situation. The state of California was the first state to allow decisions for a natural death to be the patient's choice alone. The Living Will (see appendix), which is not legally binding in most states, can provide a basis for discussion with older students of the decisions modern technology forces upon them.

To accept these decisions responsibly, the older student needs to know something about the grief process, so reactions and opinions of family members can be understood. The student also needs to know the legal restraints under which the physician works, medical definitions of death, and the most frequently used methods of "heroic" resuscitation and their desirability in various situations. Students should be encouraged to explore their feelings about organ donation and autopsy as well as the application of extreme medical measures. As in the second goal, assignments can be given that encourage students to communicate with their families in order to establish a basis for decision before the crisis time. Young children will probably not be included in these decisions, but they need to understand the reasons why family members are institutionalized and the difficulties their parents may have in making such decisions.

Most of us are unfamiliar with the funeral industry. We find in our teaching—even at the graduate level—that few students have ever been inside a funeral home, and of these only a minority have been in a casket showroom. Yet these same people could at any time be called on to buy the goods and services that the funeral industry provides, which average about $2,000 and could run far more. Students need to learn about the services that the funeral director can provide both to family and community.

A good place to begin is a cross-cultural or historic study of corpse disposal. Students should study corpse decomposition under various conditions and the legal restraints on funeral directors and their customers. With this information, visits to local mortuaries or talks with funeral directors are strongly recommended. Most funeral directors will be very pleased to arrange for a tour of their establishments at a time convenient to them. Teachers might also want to explore alternatives available through the Planned Funeral and Memorial Society in their community. Students can then explore their own values and be given assignments that encourage them to communicate with family members about funeral traditions or about what family members desire for themselves.

Evaluation

If this goal has been reached, the students should be able to show where to find appropriate information on funeral and medical services and demonstrate a knowledge of choices available. Students should be able to discuss the decisions they will have to make in the future and show that they have clarified the values according to which they and their families will make those decisions.

GOAL FOUR: To help the student formulate socioethical issues related to death and define value judgments these issues raise.

An underlying, but seldom spoken, assumption of much of the death education movement is that Americans handle death and dying poorly and that we ought to be doing better at it. As with many other things, many Americans believe that education can initiate change.

We feel that teachers need to be careful here, especially if—upon self-examination—they find that their own ideas about social change are too idealistic or too far from the mainstream for ready acceptance at this time. Rather, there are important questions of social policy and ethical practice that deserve inquiry. Teachers will best serve their students by presenting the socioethical issues in well-formulated questions and admitting that none of them yield easy answers. There are many issues that relate to death facing our culture. The following are questions of current social interest for the teacher to think about:

1. Given limited medical and economic resources, should great effort be made to maintain the lives of old people functioning at extremely low levels?

2. What is our definition of life? Do we consider length of life (quantity) more important than high-level functioning (quality) for a limited time?

3. Is the continuing trend toward private mourning rituals consistent with creating and maintaining caring communities?

4. What is the social significance of viewing artificially restored corpses?

5. Does preserving the corpse in concrete vaults, thus preventing natural decomposition, run counter to the current emphasis on ecology, and should burial alternatives be considered?

6. Is the designation of one grave plot in perpetuity for each corpse a good use of the remaining open space in our land?

7. Should a "Living Will" be legally binding?

8. How does an individual exercise personal rights under institutional care?

The teacher can reformulate these questions to match the grade level and emotional maturity of the students. Each of these issues is multifaceted and deserves careful exploration. But such exploration can only be done when the issues are clearly defined. If teachers wish to engage in social and ethical issues, they should concentrate on specific questions such as the foregoing rather than engaging in discussion without a focus.

If teachers are to be fair with their students, they must have a firm grasp of the complexity of the issues involved, for unexamined assumptions will bias the presentation by allowing the teacher's unexamined values to appear as fact to the students. This puts the students at a decided disadvantage when they are ready to consider the questions themselves.

By the junior high school level, students are ready—when they have been prepared by the information in the first goal—to conduct debates, readings, and discussions on these basic questions of social policy. Today's students have been sensitized enough ecologically to appreciate the problems of the use of open space for burial or the preservation and storage of human bodies.

As the older students study almost any aspect of death and dying, they will make judgments about these social questions. The teacher can help facilitate social change by placing the students in the best possible context with sufficient information for making these judgments. Many of these issues are now being raised in the culture at large, so teachers might do well to watch for media events and recent publications that can be used as a basis for discussion.

Evaluation

This evaluation has two parts: (1) Students should be able to demonstrate knowledge about the various facets of socioethical issues related to death and dying. (2) They should be able to articulate the particular value system within which they make their decisions.

ENRICHING
DEATH EDUCATION

Some of what is now being done in the name of death education does not fit in with the foregoing goals but rather is concerned with aesthetic enrichment in the study of literature, art, or philosophy as they reflect death themes. Many of the publications about death in the education journals are lists of good novels or short stories that start the student thinking about death or that have a certain viewpoint the student might use. If we were to state the goal toward which this kind of teaching is directed, it would be: "To gain literary, philosophical, or artistic insight using the human experience of death as a focus." Such teaching is surely a worthwhile activity, for it is from art, religion, literature, and philosophy that we gain the more profound insights that make our living and dying richer.

This kind of death education serves best as enrichment of the more basic goals already outlined. Our students will be equipped to confront the creative minds of our culture as those minds reflect on death when the students have first reflected on it themselves. Especially in the higher grades, it is too easy to substitute knowledge from books and the mastery of argument for knowledge of real life and death and the mastery of living. The problems our students face are ignorance of basic facts in their world, the inability to deal with death when confronted by it, the lack of background to make basic consumer decisions, and the lack of value concepts to deal with the social and ethical issues death presents. Death is part of art and literature because it is part of life. It seems more realistic that the students begin to study life experiences first and then aesthetic enrichment. We have included enrichment materials in the curriculum that the teacher will be able to use within the four suggested goals.

FURTHER READING

GREEN, BETTY, and DONALD IRISH, *Death Education: Preparation for Living*. Cambridge, Mass.: Schenkman Publishing Co., 1971.

LEVITON, DANIEL, "The Scope of Death Education," *Death Education*, 1:1 (Spring 1977), 41–56.

MILLS, GRETCHEN C., and others, *Discussing Death: A Guide to Death Education*. Homewood, Ill.: ETC Publications, 1976.

STANFORD, GENE, and DEBORAH PERRY, *Death Out of the Closet*. New York: Bantam Books, 1976.

This section is a guide for teachers as they plan their lessons in death education. It is by no means exhaustive; that is, we do not list everything that can be done. Teachers know their own students and their own teaching strengths, so the suggestions we make should be adopted to each teacher's style and student needs.

We have arranged curriculum suggestions by grade level and by the goals we discussed in Chapter 6. Teachers should read the chapter on goals carefully and decide for themselves which goal or goals they want to use. They can then find that goal under the appropriate grade level where curriculum is outlined. If that goal does not exist as a unit in the grade level the teacher needs, we suggest that the curriculum for grade levels just above or below the students' level be considered for adaptation, especially if

Suggested Curricula by Grade and Goal

Chapter **7**

there has been little other death education in the school.

Each curriculum unit is centered around one or more objectives that are more specific statements of the general goal. A list of resources that are available for the teacher and for the students follows. Student resources have been selected for accuracy and relative absence of judgmental value statements. Some student resources we reviewed were misleading or simply not well done, and these were not included; but our omissions do not automatically carry a negative evaluation. We make no claim to have found every book or audio-visual aid there is, and even as we are writing, more good curriculum resources are being developed; so teachers should not feel limited by what we suggest. There is almost no perfect resource, so although there may be some problems with those cited, they are the resources we would be willing to use ourselves.

Teacher resources provide information and background suitable for adults to prepare themselves for discussion and teaching of the specific objectives stated. Recently, there has been an increase in the number of scholarly and popular works on death and dying. We have tried to winnow through these to find some of the best books or other media on each subject, so the teacher will not be confronted with a college course bibliography in each subject. We have also tried to consider availability in choosing teacher resources. Everything suggested should be in a good public or college library or can be ordered (see bibliography at the end of the chapter).

The glossary in the back of the book should be helpful in explaining any thanatological words either students or adults do not fully understand.

The Index of Curricular Objects gives an overview of the curriculum guide as a whole. The index is divided by grade and goal, and each unit is presented in much greater detail in the same order in the curriculum guide.

INDEX OF CURRICULAR OBJECTIVES

Grade	Goal 1	Goal 2	Goal 3	Goal 4
Nursery, Kindergarten, 1, (Begins on page 149.)	Explore the life cycle of plants and animals in order to introduce students to birth, life, and death as part of the same cycle.	Talk about the feelings students have when they experience loss.		
	Find out what happens to dead people and pets, and explore the cemetery.			
	Identify various stages in the life cycle with special attention to the characteristics of old age.			

2, 3 (Begins on page 155.)	Include human death within the biological life cycle. Find out what causes death.	Explore students' feelings when someone dies. Explore students' ideas of death as expressed in the culture.	Introduce funeral procedures and the funeral establishment.
4, 5 (Begins on page 162.)	Introduce the student to factual information about the demography of death. Introduce to the student the facts about institutions that are concerned with death.	Help children reflect upon their past ideas of death, and consolidate these views. (Student is in a transitional period to more mature concepts of death, and this topic will help formulate students' new ideas and acceptance of death as a final reality.) Children begin to accept the reality and finality of their own deaths.	Explore society's values on issues related to death and dying as presented in media ordinarily seen by young children.

Grade	Goal 1	Goal 2	Goal 3	Goal 4
6, 7 (Begins on page 169.)	Acquaint the students with the legal and scientific definitions of death. Students study various methods of body disposal.	Help the student develop a philosophy of life and death. Students learn the appropriate social behavior at the time of death and mourning. Maturing students identify feelings they and others have in anticipating death and feelings they might have at the time of death.	Help students clarify their value systems on the issue of body disposal.	
8, 9 (Begins on page 181.)	Cross-cultural study of beliefs and customs about death in order to acquaint students with a broad range of views and practices concerning death.	Explore the students' own feelings about the aged and getting old.	Discover the medical context of dying in modern America, and introduce the student to the technology, professional duties, and attitudes surrounding death.	Introduce the students to basic ethical and social policy issues connected with dying.

8, 9 (cont.)	Understand the dynamics of aging and death and the social institutions that deal with them. Explore attitudes and stereotypes about aging in America.		
10, 11 (Begins on page 190.)	Acquaint the student with current legal and medical definitions of death, and introduce the problematic character of those definitions. Acquaint students with the legalities and problems of body and organ donation.	Make students aware of their response to loss and ways of coping with that loss. Have the students explore decisions about death and dying as these decisions would affect them and their families.	Acquaint students with the financial aspects of medical care for terminal illness and life-threatening situations. Introduce the student to a variety of methods of body disposal, current funeral practice, and relative costs.	Acquaint the student with the legal and moral issues reflected in the problems of the prolongation of life and the termination of life.

Grade	Goal 1	Goal 2	Goal 3	Goal 4
12 (Begins on page 199.)	Survey theories about suicide and its occurrence in our culture.	Have students explore their own feelings about suicide.	Acquaint students with insurance and wills.	
		Acquaint the student with experiences connected with the crises of death and dying that may not fit into commonly accepted reality.		

SUGGESTED CURRICULA

GRADES: Nursery School, Kindergarten, 1

GOAL ONE: To inform the students of facts not currently widespread in the culture.

OBJECTIVE: To explore the life cycle of plants and animals in order to introduce students to birth, life, and death as part of the same cycle.

ACTIVITIES

1. Bring plant materials to class (i.e., buds, seeds, vegetables, dried flowers, leaves, and so forth); discuss and observe the complete life cycles of plants—the class can plant seeds and nonliving materials and compare results.

2. After reading stories, have a discussion about dead animals children observe in everyday life: (a) What is dead? (b) Why do animals die? (c) What happens to the body? (d) In what ways are people like animals?

3. If there are any pets in the classroom, teacher can give the class the life-cycle information for each kind of pet.

4. Children can share their experience with family pets.

STUDENT RESOURCES

READING*

Warburg, Sandol, *Growing Time*. Boston: Houghton Mifflin, 1969. Sensitive story of death and burial of family pet and what happens to the pet when he's buried.

*Note on obtaining materials: If any books or media prove hard to find, Highly Specialized Promotions (P. O. Box 989, GPO, Brooklyn, N.Y. 11201) specializes in thanatology materials and is helpful in locating and placing special orders for what is not in stock.

Brown, Margaret Wise, *The Dead Bird*. Glenview, Ill.: Scott Foresman, 1965. Children find dead bird and conduct burial services for it.

Tressalt, Alvin, *The Dead Tree*. New York: Parents Magazine Press, 1971. An old oak tree comes to the end of its life cycle and decays to fertilize the soil for another plant and for the sprouting acorns of new oaks.

Stull, Edith, *My Turtle Died Today*. New York: Holt, Rinehart & Winston, 1964. A matter-of-fact presentation about a dying turtle, his death, his burial by children, and the new kittens of the family cat representing the life cycle of birth and death.

OTHER MEDIA

"Life–Death" (filmstrip) in *Understanding Death Series*. De Kalb, Ill.: Educational Perspectives Associates, n. d. Normalcy of death for all living things.

TEACHER RESOURCES

READING

Anthony, Sylvia, *The Discovery of Death in Childhood and After*. New York: Basic Books, 1972. Classic study.

Grollman, Earl, *Talking About Death: A Dialogue Between Children and Parents*. Boston: Beacon Press, 1976. Exploration of feelings at a death.

Pringle, Laurence, *Death Is Natural*. New York: Four Winds Press, 1977. Written as a book for older children but not suitable for use by children; good scientific material for teacher to adapt, complete ecocycle of death to life described.

OBJECTIVES: To find out what happens to dead people and pets and to explore the cemetery.

Visit to cemetery or pet cemetery. Questions to ask:
1. Explain the purpose of a cemetery.
2. What is the purpose of a grave marker?
3. What happens under the ground?
4. Why do people visit cemeteries?
5. If flowers or other grave decorations are present, discuss their meaning.
6. Look at the different kinds of grave markers and the information recorded on them. Does it tell anything about the person or pet buried there?

STUDENT RESOURCES

READING

(See Student Resources for the previous objective also.)

Kantrowitz, Mildred, *When Violet Died*. New York: Parents Magazine Press, 1973. Friends join in a funeral service for a dead bird.

Viorst, Judith, *The Tenth Good Thing About Barney*. New York: Atheneum, 1971. The tenth good thing about Barney is that his body feeds the garden. Very well done.

TEACHER RESOURCES

READING

(See previous Teacher Resources as well.)

Williams, Melvin, *The Last Word, Lure and Lore of Early New England Cemeteries*. Boston: Oldston Enterprises, 1973.

Jacobs, C. Walker, *Stranger Stop and Cast An Eye: A Guide to Gravestones and Rubbings*. Brattleboro, Vt.: Stephen Greene Press, 1968.

GOAL TWO: To help the student affectively deal with the idea of personal death and the deaths of significant others.

OBJECTIVE: To identify various stages in the life cycle with special attention to the characteristics of old age.

ACTIVITIES

1. Have child cut out pictures of people of different ages from magazines or ask family for photos of the same family member at different ages; child prepares chart or collage, and teacher and child discuss the different characteristics the child identifies with the aging process.
2. Read stories about the interaction between young and old. Discuss topics such as: Who do you know that's old? How do you know they're old? How old are they?
3. Have the children discuss among themselves the oldest person they know. Identify what they perceive old people as able and not able to do. (The teacher may want to distinguish the limitations of age from the limitations of disease.)

STUDENT RESOURCES

READING
Silverstein, Shel, *The Giving Tree.* New York: Harper & Row, 1970. Beautiful relationship between a man and a tree from youth to old age.

Miles, Miska, *Annie and the Old One.* Boston: Little, Brown, 1971. Navajo grandmother faces death, saying, "Earth from which all good things come is where all creatures finally go."

Zolotow, Charlotte, *My Grandson Lew*. New York: Harper & Row, 1974. Mother and son comfort each other with shared memories of dead grandfather.

TEACHER RESOURCES

READING

Butler, Robert, *Why Survive? Being Old in America*. New York: Harper & Row, 1975. Pulitzer prize winner.

Percy, Charles, and Charles Mangel, *Growing Old in the Country of the Young*. New York: McGraw-Hill, 1974.

Curtin, Sharon, *Nobody Ever Died of Old Age*. Boston: Little, Brown, 1973. Subtitled "In Praise of Old People, in Outrage at Their Loneliness."

Blue, Gladys F., "The Aging As Portrayed in Realistic Fiction for Children 1945–1975," *The Gerontologist*, 18, No. 2 (April 1978), 187–192.

OBJECTIVE: To talk about the feelings students have when they experience loss. Feelings and behaviors such as: sadness, loneliness, wanting to cry, feeling sick, not hungry, not wanting to play, not wanting to talk, and so on.

ACTIVITIES

1. Storytelling and discussion. Guidelines for discussion:

   a. What did the people in the book feel?

   b. What made them feel that way?

    c. Have you ever felt that way, and what happened to cause those feelings?

    d. Has what happened in the story ever happened to you? How did you feel when it did?

2. Role play different emotions and body movements to express feelings. Sing songs in which death is mentioned.

STUDENT RESOURCES

READING

Berger, Terry, *I Have Feelings*. New York: Human Sciences Press, 1971. Feelings, positive and negative, in photos of the four-to-eight-year-old.

Stein, Sara, *About Dying*. New York: Walker and Co., 1974. Sensitive book about experiences with death in the young child's life—the death of a bird and the death of a grandfather and the feelings that result from these encounters. Read with child as a one-to-one dialogue (with notes for adult).

Viorst, Judith, *The Tenth Good Thing About Barney*. New York: Atheneum, 1971. Beautiful story of how child comes to terms with the death of Barney the cat.

Warburg, Sandol, *Growing Time*. Boston: Houghton Mifflin, 1969. Jamie mourns the death of the family pet and learns that "the spirit of something you really love can never die."

OTHER MEDIA

"Moods and Emotions": Eight prints (color) showing full range of children's emotions (with teacher's manual). The Child's World, P.O. Box 681, Elgin, Ill. 60120.

Songs: "Go Tell Aunt Rhody," "There Was an Old Lady

Who Swallowed a Fly," "Boa Constrictor," "Who Killed Cock Robin," many others.

TEACHER RESOURCES

READING

Nagy, Maria, "Child's View of Death" in *The Meaning of Death*, ed. Herman Feifel. New York: McGraw-Hill, 1959.

OTHER MEDIA

Children's Conceptions of Death (video recording). Milwaukee, Wis.: University of Wisconsin School of Nursing, 1974. Straightforward description of the different stages children go through in their development of concepts of death. Available for rental.

Barman, Alicerose, *Helping Children Face Crises* (pamphlet #541). New York: Public Affairs Pamphlets, n.d. Available at 381 Park Avenue South, New York, N.Y. 10010.

GRADES: 2, 3

GOAL ONE: To inform the students of facts not currently widespread in the culture.

OBJECTIVE: To include human death within the biological life cycle.

ACTIVITIES

Simulation and role playing, using coordinated filmstrip, "Playing Dead." Reading and discussion of stories. Guidelines for discussion:

1. How can we talk about other things (in nature, mechanical, and so forth) that die that compare with the

reasons for human death? (See especially *Why Did He Die?* by Audrey Harris.)

2. Does anything not die?
3. What are the characteristics of life?
4. What are the characteristics of death? (Here teacher can bring in shells, fossils, dried plants, and the like and contrast them with living matter.)
5. Make a closed ecosystem and observe (fish, plants, water, snails, and the like in a closed bottle).

STUDENT RESOURCES

READING

Smith, Doris, *A Taste of Blackberries*. New York: Thomas Y. Crowell, 1973. Same as the filmstrip in book form.

Zolotow, Charlotte, *My Grandson Lew*. New York: Harper & Row, 1974. Mother and son comfort each other with shared memories of dead grandfather.

Harris, Audrey, *Why Did He Die?* Minneapolis, Minn.: Lerner Press, 1965. Death of a grandfather is compared with an autumn season and with worn machinery.

De Paola, Tomie, *Nana Upstairs and Nana Downstairs*. East Rutherford, N.J.: Putnam's, 1973. Comprehensive look at aging and the inevitability of death.

OTHER MEDIA

Hall, Carol, "It's All Right to Cry," in *Free to Be You and Me Songbook* by Marlo Thomas and Friends. New York: McGraw-Hill, 1974. Also as a record, Bell Records (1110 Stereo), 1972.

"A Taste of Blackberries" (filmstrip) in *Understanding Death Series*. De Kalb, Ill.: Educational Perspectives Associates, n.d. Beautiful story of boy coming to terms with death of a friend. Available at P.O. Box 213, De Kalb, Ill. 60115.

"Playing Dead" (filmstrip) in *Understanding Changes in the Family*. Pleasantville, N.Y.: Guidance Associates, n.d. Opportunity for child to air emotions and fantasies about death.

TEACHER RESOURCES

READING

Anthony, Sylvia, *The Discovery of Death in Childhood and After*. New York: Basic Books, 1972.

Pringle, Laurence, *Death Is Natural*. New York: Four Winds Press, 1977. Written as a book for older children but not suitable for use by children; good scientific material for teacher to adapt, complete ecocycle of death to life described.

OBJECTIVE: To find out what causes death.

ACTIVITIES

1. Students cut out and make a collage or scrapbook using newspapers, magazines, whatever, on things that cause death. Family members can also provide information for student.

2. Students display and discuss collected materials in class. Teacher can make a bulletin board on "Causes of Death."

3. Teacher provides students with:

   a. facts about life expectancy and how it has changed over the years;

b. what people used to die from (communicable diseases, accidents, childbirth, and so forth);

c. leading causes of death today.

STUDENT RESOURCES

Magazines, newspapers, comic books.

TEACHER RESOURCES

READING

Lerner, Monroe, "When, Why and Where People Die," in *Death: Current Perspectives*, ed. Edwin Shneidman. Palo Alto, Calif.: Mayfield Publishers, 1976. Demography of death.

Schulz, Richard, *The Psychology of Death, Dying and Bereavement*. Reading, Mass.: Addison-Wesley, 1978. Excellent chapter (3) on causes of death and demography of death.

GOAL TWO: To help the student affectively deal with the idea of personal death and deaths of significant others.

OBJECTIVE: To explore students' feelings when someone dies.

ACTIVITIES

1. Discussion based on student resources and guidelines suggested in teacher's manual for "A Taste of Blackberries" (filmstrip) and stories read to class (see K–1 for other stories).

2. Class learns songs, "It's All Right to Cry" or "Every-

body Cries Sometimes," and draws pictures of times when crying is appropriate.

STUDENT RESOURCES

READING

(See prior Student Resources as well.)

Warburg, Sandol, *Growing Time.* Boston: Houghton Mifflin, 1969.

Viorst, Judith, *The Tenth Good Thing About Barney.* New York: Atheneum, 1971.

LeShan, Eda, *Learning to Say Good-by, When a Parent Dies.* New York: Macmillan, 1976.

OTHER MEDIA

(See prior Student Resources as well.)

"Everybody Cries Sometimes" (record) with song lyrics included. Educational Activities, Inc., P.O. Box 392, Freeport, N.Y. 11520.

The Street (motion picture; 10 minutes, color). Animated cartoon showing small child's response to final sickness and death of grandmother living in the house. Excellent at depicting feelings. Available from Audio Visual Education Center, University of Michigan, 416 Fourth Street, Ann Arbor, Michigan 48103.

TEACHER RESOURCES

READING

Grollman, Earl, *Talking About Death: A Dialogue Between Parent and Child.* Boston: Beacon Press, 1970.

Pincus, Lily, *Death in the Family.* New York: Random House, 1974.

Jackson, Edgar, *Telling a Child About Death*. New York: Hawthorn, Inc., 1965.

Ramos, Suzanne, *Teaching Your Child to Cope with Crisis*. New York: McKay, 1974.

OBJECTIVE: To explore students' ideas of death expressed in the culture.

ACTIVITY

Have children draw their idea of what death is. Teacher can bring in common cultural symbols of death (e.g., Grim Reaper, Angels, Mushroom Clouds, Skull and Crossbones, Darth Vadar). Discuss meaning of pictures with children. This is an age when children begin to see personifications of death, and the teacher is making explicit that which is part of normal fantasy life.

STUDENT RESOURCES

Use films, comics, magazines, books, and so forth.

TEACHER RESOURCES

READING

Kastenbaum, Robert, *Death, Society and Human Experience*. St. Louis, Mo.: C.V. Mosby, 1977. Chapter 4.

Lerner, E., and I. Lerner, compilers, *Devils, Demons, Death and Damnation*. New York: Dover, 1971. Medieval and Renaissance views of death, evil, and afterlife.

Nagy, Maria, "The Child's View of Death," in *The Meaning of Death*, ed. Herman Feifel. New York: McGraw-Hill, 1959.

GOAL THREE: To make the student an informed consumer of medical and funeral services.

OBJECTIVE: To introduce funeral procedures and the funeral establishment.

ACTIVITY

Class visits funeral home. Teacher should visit funeral home first to familiarize self with surroundings and objects. Read teacher resources, and be able to present explanations of basic funeral customs and what the students will see when they visit. Teacher ought to insure that there are no bodies present during class visit. Read *Tell Me About Death, Tell Me About Funerals* to class as preparation for funeral home visit.

STUDENT RESOURCES

READING

Corley, Elizabeth, *Tell Me About Death, Tell Me About Funerals*. Santa Clara, Calif.: Grammatical Sciences, 1973.

Lee, Virginia, *The Magic Moth*. New York: Seabury Press, Inc., 1972. Butterfly becomes symbol of hope, and funeral process is well explained.

TEACHER RESOURCES

READING

Habenstein, Robert, and William Lamers, *The History of American Funeral Directing*. Milwaukee, Wis.: Bulfin Printers, Inc., 1962.

———, *Funeral Customs the World Over* (3rd rev. ed.). Milwaukee, Wis.: Radtke Brothers and Kortsch, 1974.

Pine, Vanderlyn, *Caretaker of the Dead: The American Funeral Director*. New York: Irvington Publishers, 1975.

Local funeral directors will have available free, industry-prepared publications explaining their services.

GRADES: 4, 5

GOAL ONE: To inform the students of facts not currently widespread in the culture.

OBJECTIVE: To introduce the student to factual information about the demography of death.

ACTIVITIES

1. Reading, discussion, and preparation of charts and statistics on the demography of death (Bureau of Vital Statistics may be able to provide information).

2. After reading *Life and Death*, chart life span of various species.

3. Look up life spans of important historical figures, and ask whether life span was a determinant to a person's achieving fame. If possible, find out the life spans of other people in the famous person's family to see if there was a heredity factor operating for longevity.

4. Before reading, class writes down things they believe about causes of death and ages when people die. After reading student resources, class rechecks their beliefs against factual information they have learned. Discuss why the students may have had some misconceptions about the demography of death.

READING

Corley, Elizabeth, *Tell Me About Death, Tell Me About Funerals*. Santa Clara, Calif.: Grammatical Sciences, 1973.

Klein, Stanley, *The Final Mystery*. New York: Doubleday, 1974. Chapter 4, "The War Against Death."

Zim, Herbert, and Sonia Bleeker, *Life and Death*. New York: Morrow, 1970. Answers to questions about physical facts, customs, and attitudes about death.

TEACHER RESOURCES

READING

Kastenbaum, Robert, and Ruth Aisenberg, *The Psychology of Death*. New York: Springer, 1972. See Chapters 2, 3, and 8.

Lerner, Monroe, "When, Why and Where People Die," in *Death: Current Perspectives*, ed. Edwin Schneidman. Palo Alto, Calif.: Mayfield Publishing, 1976.

Schulz, Richard, *The Psychology of Death, Dying and Bereavement*. Reading, Mass.: Addison-Wesley, 1978. Chapter 3, "The Demography of Death."

Life and Death and Medicine. San Francisco: W. H. Freeman, 1973. Book form of special issue of *Scientific American*.

OBJECTIVE: To introduce the student to the facts about institutions that are concerned with death.

ACTIVITY

Teacher presents different locales where death may take place, providing information about each: hospital, nursing home, hospice, home.

OTHER MEDIA

Dignity of Death (motion picture; 30 minutes, color). New York: ABC News, n.d. Story of St. Christopher's Hospice and its staff's humane treatment of the dying. Available at 7 W. 66th St., New York, N.Y. 10023.

Peege (motion picture). New York: Phoenix Films, 1974. Boy tries to communicate with grandmother isolated in nursing home. Available for rent from Visual-Aid Service, University of Illinois, 1352 So. Oak, Champaign, Ill. 61820.

TEACHER RESOURCES

READING

Mauksch, Hans, "The Organizational Context of Dying," in *Death: The Final Stage of Growth*, ed. Elisabeth Kübler–Ross. Englewood Cliffs, N.J.: Prentice-Hall, 1975.

Neale, Robert, "Between the Nipple and the Everlasting Arms," in *Death and Society*, eds. James Carse and Arlene Dallery. New York: Harcourt Brace Jovanovich, 1977.

Saunders, Cicely, "Dying They Live: St. Christopher's Hospice," in *New Meanings of Death*, ed. Herman Feifel. New York: McGraw-Hill, 1977.

Sudnow, David, *Passing On*. Englewood Cliffs, N.J.: Prentice-Hall, 1967.

GOAL TWO: To help the student affectively deal with the idea of personal death and the deaths of significant others.

OBJECTIVE: To help children reflect upon their past ideas of death and consolidate these views. Student is in a transitional period to more mature concepts of death, and this will help formulate student's new ideas and acceptance of death as a final reality.

ACTIVITIES

1. Show films and have class read material from earlier grades and discuss how their ideas have changed.
2. Have class discuss whether cartoons portray life and death in a realistic fashion.
3. Students discuss past experiences with death and how they remember feeling at the time.
4. Writing assignment of earliest death-related experiences; have students evaluate present position as compared to earlier grades. (This includes experiences of death of pets.)
5. Sing nursery rhymes and school yard chants about death. Discuss why students like to sing them and what they might mean in terms of relieving anxieties and fears about death. Teacher might share his or her own childhood chants, games, and memories.

STUDENT RESOURCES

READING
Use a selection of stories from grades K–3, especially those you know have been used in your school before.

OTHER MEDIA
Chants and rhymes: "Rockabye Baby," "Ring Around the Rosie," "London Bridge Is Falling Down," "Did You Ever See a Hearse Go By?" many others.

"Playing Dead" (filmstrip) in *Understanding Changes in the*

Family. Pleasantville, N.Y.: Guidance Associates, n.d. Shows feelings of very young children.

Where Is Dead? (motion picture; 19 minutes, color). Chicago: Encyclopedia Britannica Films, n.d. Impact of brother's death on six-year-old girl, sensitively presented. Available at 425 N. Michigan, Chicago, Ill. 60611.

Any cartoons that show the character to be indestructible or immortal.

TEACHER RESOURCES

READING

Nagy, Maria, "Child's View of Death," in *The Meaning of Death*, ed. Herman Feifel. New York: McGraw-Hill, 1959.

Bakan, David, *The Slaughter of the Innocents.* San Francisco: Jossey-Bass, 1971.

Bettelheim, Bruno, *The Uses of Enchantment.* New York: Knopf, 1976.

OTHER MEDIA

Children's Conceptions of Death (video recording). Milwaukee, Wis.: University of Wisconsin School of Nursing, 1974. Available for sale or rental.

OBJECTIVE: To help children accept the reality and finality of their own deaths.

ACTIVITIES

These activities are designed to deal with the feelings that the concept of mortality raises.

1. Use a sentence-completion exercise: "Death is like. . . ." "A good thing about death is. . . . " "The

scariest thing about death is. . . . " "Death will happen when. . . . " and others the teacher can provide. Teacher can point out commonality of fears and that it is natural to fear the unknown.

2. Children read fiction books listed in resources or others they may choose about people dying.

3. Writing poetry, music, and creative art activities are also good ways to have students express feelings.

STUDENT RESOURCES

READING

Carlson, Natalie, *The Half Sisters*. New York: Harper & Row, 1970. Girl copes with death of a sister.

Erdman, Lolla, *A Bluebird Will Do*. New York: Dodd, Mead, 1973. About the death of a parent.

Lorenzo, Carol Lee, *Mama's Ghosts*. New York: Harper & Row, 1974. Dying grandmother helps young girl understand that sometimes we must say good-bye to those we love, even though it hurts.

Watts, Richard, *Straight Talk About Death with Young People*. Philadelphia: Westminster Press, 1975.

White, E. B., *Charlotte's Web*. New York: Harper & Row, 1952.

TEACHER RESOURCES

READING

Kübler–Ross, Elisabeth, *On Death and Dying*. New York: Macmillan, 1969.

Steven, Joseph, *Children in Fear*. New York: Holt, Rinehart

& Winston, 1974. Children reveal the many ways we teach them fear of death, sex, and fear itself.

Wahl, C. W. "Fear of Death," in *The Meaning of Death*, ed. Herman Feifel. New York: McGraw-Hill, 1959.

OTHER MEDIA

Living With Dying—Part I (filmstrip). Pound Ridge, N.Y.: Sunburst Communications, 1972. Looks for reasons for man's death as well as attempts to cheat death through searches for immortality.

GOAL FOUR: To help the student formulate socioethical issues related to death and define value judgments these issues raise.

OBJECTIVE: To explore society's values on issues related to death and dying as presented in media ordinarily seen by young children.

ACTIVITY

Determine by survey what students most commonly watch on television or read in comic books. Assign students to watch the most popular programs in one specific time period. (Teachers must also watch and prepare discussion questions.) Questions to be discussed:

1. To whom does death occur? What kind of characters die?
2. How does death occur?
3. Is death related to concepts of good and evil? Are good deeds rewarded with life and bad deeds punished by death?

4. Is death presented realistically?

5. Is the reality of death denied?

6. Does TV mirror the student's life experience?

7. Are any concepts of afterlife common in our culture?

8. How are these concepts related to social values?

STUDENT RESOURCES

If possible, videotape one or two programs so that the entire class can see them together. It is also possible to rent cartoons or use comic books the students are reading.

TEACHER RESOURCES

READING

Kastenbaum, Robert, *Death, Society and Human Experience*. St. Louis: C. V. Mosby, 1977. Chapter 4.

GRADES: 6, 7

GOAL ONE: To inform the students of facts not currently widespread in the culture.

OBJECTIVE: To acquaint the students with the legal and scientific definitions of death.

ACTIVITIES

1. Learn traditional and emerging definitions of death. Bring blood pressure cuff, feather, stethoscope, thermometer, mirror, flashlight, and reflex hammer to class if possible, and have students find vital signs

of life and reflex action. (Ask school nurse or doctor to help you find items. See if you can get EEG and EKG tracings from your local hospital.)

2. Learn legal procedures for certification of death.

   a. Have students look at family death certificates and bring reports of primary and secondary causes.

   b. Trace routes of certificate.

   c. Outline types of cases with which medical examiner's office becomes involved; check with local hospital for regulations they must follow in reporting to coroner's office or medical examiner.

   d. Ask physician to talk on certifying death and vital signs.

STUDENT RESOURCES

READING

Black, Henry Campbell, *Black's Law Dictionary* (4th ed.). St. Paul, Minn.: West Publishing Co., 1968. Look up definitions of death.

Zim, Herbert, and Sonia Bleeker, *Life and Death.* New York: Morrow, 1970, 63 pp. Survey of life functions, medical tests, and so forth (also suitable for Goal 3).

OTHER MEDIA

"Harvard Medical School Definition of Brain Death" (see appendix).

Copy of local death certificate; physicians, funeral directors, hospitals, and medical examiners have them (see appendix).

READING

Hendin, David, *Death as a Fact of Life*. New York: Norton, 1973, Chapter 1.

Mant, Keith, "The Medical Definition of Death," in *Death: Current Perspectives*, ed. Edwin Schneidman. Palo Alto, Calif.: Mayfield Publishing Co., 1976.

Veatch, Robert, "Brain Death," in *Death: Current Perspectives*, ed. Edwin Schneidman. Palo Alto, Calif.: Mayfield Publishing Co., 1976.

Veatch, Robert, *Death, Dying and the Biological Revolution*. New Haven, Conn.: Yale University Press, 1976, Chapters 1 and 2. Difficult reading, but the definitive work in the field.

OBJECTIVE: Students study the various methods of body disposal.

ACTIVITIES

1. Visit a funeral home and cemetery, family graves, mausoleum, columbarium.
2. Ask a funeral director about methods of body disposition.
3. Talk to a physician about organ donation and body donation.
4. Students talk to parents and grandparents about funeral customs in their family and prepare reports in the form of a book, scrapbook, recording, and the like.

5. Students research funeral customs in past and other cultures. Make bulletin board, class newspaper, spend class time in school library.

STUDENT RESOURCES

READING

Coffin, Margaret, *Death in Early America: History and Folklore of Customs and Superstitions of Early Medicine, Funerals, Burial and Mourning*. Nashville, Tenn.: Thomas Nelson, 1976.

Habenstein, Robert, and William Lamers, *Funeral Customs the World Over*. Milwaukee, Wis.: Bulfin Printers, Inc., 1960.

Wallis, Charles, *American Epitaphs, Grave and Humorous*. New York: Dover, 1973.

Funeral trade magazine, *Casket and Sunnyside*. Obtainable from funeral directors.

Use encyclopedias and reference materials.

OTHER MEDIA:

"A Time to Mourn—A Time to Choose" in *Death and Dying: Closing the Circle*. Pleasantville, N.Y.: Guidance Associates, 1975. An excellent filmstrip showing many alternatives for disposal of body and funeral rituals.

The Great American Funeral (motion picture). Focuses on the economic nature of the funeral industry, but cost and funeral styles are outdated. Still good to illustrate funeral industry's services and Forest Lawn Cemetery in California. Available from Mass Media, 1720 Chouteau, St. Louis, Mo. 63103.

READING

Aries, Philippe, *Western Attitudes Toward Death*. Baltimore, Md.: Johns Hopkins University Press, 1974.

Arvio, Raymond, *The Cost of Dying and What You Can Do About It*. New York: Harper & Row, 1974.

Habenstein, Robert, and William Lamers, *History of American Funeral Directing*. Milwaukee, Wis.: Bulfin Printers, Inc., 1962. Look at chapter headings and read selectively.

Mann, Thomas, and Janet Greene, *Over Their Dead Bodies: Yankee Epitaphs and History*. Brattleboro, Vt.: Stephen Greene Press, 1962.

Morgan, Ernest, *Manual for Death Education and Simple Burial*. Burnsville, N.C.: Celo Press, 1977. From planned funeral and memorial society's point of view. Order from Alternatives, 701 North Eugene St., Greensboro, N.C., 27401 or Continental Association of Funeral and Memorial Societies (see following for address). Excellent resource suitable for students' use as well.

Pine, Vanderlyn, *Caretaker of the Dead: The American Funeral Director*. New York: Irvington Publishers, 1975.

Continental Association of Funeral and Memorial Societies, Suite 1100, 1828 L St., N.W., Washington, D.C. 20036. Information on preplanned funeral and memorial societies.

Otero, G., "Death as a Part of Life: An Experimental Unit." ERIC Document Reproduction Service No. ED 128 262. Report on cross-cultural study of death customs; includes handouts and sources.

GOAL TWO: To help the student affectively deal with the idea of personal death and the deaths of significant others.

OBJECTIVE: To help the student develop a philosphy of life and death.

ACTIVITIES

1. Invite clergy to discuss particular meaning systems of life and death.
2. Read essays and poetry, and listen to music. Discussion may be based on student resources and materials from other areas of study (English, drama, music).
3. Students write creative essays on their attempts to give meaning to death.
4. Students write eulogies about their own lives as they wish to be remembered if they were to die at age twenty, thirty, forty, fifty and so on. Students research eulogies delivered for famous persons: John Kennedy, Abraham Lincoln, Winston Churchill.
5. Consult clergy on what they feel is important about the eulogy.

STUDENT RESOURCES

READING
Armstrong, William, *Sour Land*. New York: Harper & Row, 1971. The boy in "Sounder," now old, helps three white children to understand death, injustice, and indignity.

Ball, Geraldine, "I See Death This Way" (art project) and "Death in Major and Minor" (music appreciation) in *Innerchange* (junior high). La Mesa, Calif.: Human Development Training Institute, Inc., 1977. Units with worksheets for students. Entire series on death available from 7574 University Ave., La Mesa, Calif. 92041 or call (toll free) (800) 854-2166.

Benchley, Nathaniel, *Only Earth and Sky Last Forever*. New York: Harper & Row, 1972. A young Cherokee whose beloved dies loses hope for the survival of the Indian nation.

George, Jean, *Julia of the Wolves*. New York: Harper & Row, 1972. Eskimo girl's life is saved by a wolf pack. Her sadness at the death of the pack's leader makes her aware of the disintegration of her Eskimo heritage as well.

OTHER MEDIA

Brian's Song (motion picture; 75 minutes, color). Friendship between dying football player and teammate (Brian Piccolo and Gale Sayers). Available from Learning Corp. of America, 1350 Avenue of the Americas, New York, N.Y. 10019.

Songs: "See That My Grave Is Kept Clean," Bob Dylan; "Will the Circle Be Unbroken," Mother Mabel Carter, Roy Acuff, and Friends; "Oh Death," Dock Boggs; "Paint It Black," Rolling Stones; Beatle songs, and any others that teacher and students want to use.

TEACHER RESOURCES

READING

Grollman, Earl, ed., *Concerning Death*. Boston: Beacon Press, 1974, Chapters 5, 6, and 7. Protestant, Jewish, and Catholic views of death.

OBJECTIVE: To help the students learn the appropriate social behavior at the time of death and mourning.

1. Study and comparison of obituaries and death notices (paid death advertisements); students note information provided such as wishes concerning flowers or charitable donations, time of funeral, personal accomplishments, memberships in various organizations, religious affiliation, and so on.

2. Students write obituaries, choosing subject: self, family, or famous persons. Have students read local obituaries in order to understand the local style of writing. Contrast with obituaries in national magazines or publications from other parts of the country.

3. Students interview parents and grandparents about social customs of death in their youth, including ways in which mourners received help from others.

4. Students role play appropriate social behavior and interaction at visitations, wakes, shiva, etc.

5. Students practice writing sympathy notes after a discussion of what such notes mean.

6. Visit local newspaper. Interview reporter who writes obituaries for local paper.

STUDENT RESOURCES

READING
Daily newspaper and magazines.

OTHER MEDIA
"When Someone is Grieving" (filmstrip) in *Loss and Grief*. Costa Mesa, Calif.: Concept Media, 1977. Shows things that are helpful to do for people who are grieving. Written

for professionals but can be used with young people (includes instructor's manual). Available from 1500 Adams Ave., Costa Mesa, Calif. 92626.

TEACHER RESOURCES

READING

Jackson, Edgar, *You and Your Grief.* New York: Hawthorn, 1961.

Morris, Sarah, *Grief and How to Live with It.* New York: Grosset & Dunlap, 1972.

Silverman, Phyllis, and others, *Healing Each Other in Widowhood.* New York: Health Sciences Publishing Co., 1974.

OBJECTIVE: To help maturing students identify feelings they and others have in anticipating death and feelings they might have at the time of a death.

ACTIVITIES

1. Students' class exposure to literature, drama, or art allows them to discuss the feelings of the characters and their own feelings in coping with death and dying events. (Teacher should not feel limited by our lists of readings, films, or songs.)

2. Students write an epitaph for someone else. (See resources listed elsewhere for this grade.)

3. Students write a letter to a friend about another friend who is moving away or about some recent loss they have experienced.

READING

Ball, Geraldine, *Innerchange, A Journey into Self-Learning Through Group Interaction* (junior and senior high school levels—specify which needed). Circle sessions 32a–32e and supporting activities 32f–32h. This unit provides a channel for sharing students' concepts and feelings about life and death in a nurturing social atmosphere. Worksheets for students, notes, references, resources, and guidance for teachers. Order from Human Development Training Institute, Inc., 7574 University Avenue, La Mesa, Calif. 92041, or call (toll free) (800) 854-2166.

Bernstein, Joanne, *Loss and How to Cope with It*. New York: Seabury Books, 1977.

Crawford, Charles, *Three-Legged Race*. New York: Harper & Row, 1974. Three children in a hospital become friends and become separated by both recovery and death.

Farley, Carol, *The Garden Is Doing Fine*. New York: Atheneum, 1975. Carrie's father is dying, and she is able to accept his death and how he will live on in her life.

Hunter, Mollie, *A Sound of Chariots*. New York: Harper & Row, 1972. Novel about girl dealing with the death of her father with a good interpretation of the sights and sounds of death.

Renaldo, C. L., *Dark Dreams*. New York: Harper & Row, 1974. The preadolescent search for self-acceptance, viewed through a boy who is haunted by dreams of his dead mother. Outstanding.

Whitman, Walt, "When Lilacs Last in the Dooryard Bloom'd," in many poetry anthologies.

178

OTHER MEDIA

All the Way Home (motion picture). Young boy and his mother try to cope with the death of the father. Available from Films Incorporated, 1144 Wilmette Ave., Wilmette, Ill. 60091.

"Loss" and "The Grief Process" (filmstrips) in *Loss and Grief*. Costa Mesa, Calif.: Concept Media, 1977. Good didactic lesson about feelings concerned with loss. Use first half of "The Grief Process" only. Available from 1500 Adams Ave., Costa Mesa, Calif. 92626.

TEACHER RESOURCES

READING

Becker, Ernest, *The Denial of Death*. New York: Free Press, 1973. Chapter 1 is an especially good reference for a child's feelings about death.

Grollman, Earl, ed., *Explaining Death to Children*. Boston: Beacon Press, 1967.

Jackson, Edgar, N., *Telling a Child About Death*. New York: Hawthorn, 1965.

Kübler–Ross, Elisabeth, *On Death and Dying*. New York: Macmillan, 1969.

Wahl, Charles W., "The Fear of Death," in *The Meaning of Death*, ed. Herman Feifel. New York: McGraw-Hill, 1959.

GOAL THREE: To make the student an informed consumer of medical and funeral services.

OBJECTIVE: To help students clarify their value systems on the issue of body disposal.

ACTIVITIES

1. Students answer questions relating to funerals and funeral practices from *Psychology Today* questionnaire before discussion. Tabulate and then discuss them, using resources from Goal 1. Have students answer questions again at the end of this activity, seeing if they can be more explicit about their values.

2. Teacher presents various methods and costs of body disposal:

   a. Ground burial

   b. Cremation

   c. Organ and body donation

   d. Cryonics (freezing bodies)

STUDENT RESOURCES

Local funeral directors and burial societies.

TEACHER RESOURCES

READING

Irion, Paul, *Cremation*. Philadelphia: Fortress Press, 1968.

Morgan, Ernest, *Manual for Death Education and Simple Burial*. Burnsville, N.C.: Celo Press, 1977. From planned funeral and memorial society's point of view. Order from Alternatives, 701 North Eugene St., Greensboro, N.C. 27401 or Continental Association of Funeral and Memorial Societies, Suite 1100, 1828 L Street, N.W., Washington, D.C. 20036. Teacher can get cost information from local funeral director, National Funeral Director's Association, or burial societies as listed in *Manual for Death Education and Simple Burial.*

Funeral Industry Practices—Proposed Trade Regulation and Staff Memorandum. Washington, D.C.: Federal Trade Commission, Bureau of Consumer Protection, 1975. Excellent resource, available free.

"You and Death" questionnaire in *Psychology Today* (magazine). New York: Ziff-Davis Publishing Co., August 1970.

GRADES: 8, 9

GOAL ONE: To inform the students of facts not currently widespread in the culture.

OBJECTIVE: A cross-cultural study of beliefs and customs about death in order to acquaint students with a broad range of views and practices concerning death.

ACTIVITY

Students individually or in groups research funeral customs and death beliefs of a group different from their own.

STUDENT RESOURCES

READING

Habenstein, Robert, and William Lamers, *Funeral Customs the World Over.* Milwaukee, Wis.: Bulfin Printers, 1960.

Sullivan, Walter, "The Neanderthal Man Liked Flowers," *New York Times*, June 13, 1968.

Turner, Ann Warren, *Houses for the Dead.* New York: McKay, 1976. Burial customs of ancient societies.

TEACHER RESOURCES

READING
Aries, Philippe, *Western Attitudes Toward Death*. Baltimore, Md.: Johns Hopkins University Press, 1974.

Boose, T. S., *Death in the Middle Ages*. New York: McGraw-Hill, 1972.

OBJECTIVE: To understand dynamics of aging and death and the social institutions that deal with them.

ACTIVITIES

1. Visit nursing home (have constructive activity planned for student–resident interaction). If possible to arrange regular visits throughout the semester, have students keep diary or journal of thoughts and feelings about their visits. Discuss what they learned about institutions and the aged in them.

2. Discuss how aging persons in the students' families are cared for—special needs, where they live, and so on. Identify the aged who still live, work, and function in the community.

3. Invite senior citizens to class to talk about their daily lives.

4. Discuss "A Crabbit Old Woman Wrote This" and what the "old woman" is trying to communicate (see appendix).

STUDENT RESOURCES

OTHER MEDIA
Peege (motion picture; 38 minutes, color). New York: Phoenix Films, n.d. Boy visits grandmother in nursing

home and tries to break through her isolation. Available from Phoenix Films, 420 Park Ave. South, New York, N.Y. 10016.

Songs: "Old Friends," Paul Simon; "Hello in There," John Prine; "The Dutchman," Steve Goodman; "My Old Man," Randy Newman; and many others.

TEACHER RESOURCES

(See other resources listed for this grade on aging.)

READING

Gubrium, Jaber, *Living and Dying at Murray Manor*. New York: St. Martin's, 1975.

Percy, Charles, and Charles Mangel, *Growing Old in the Country of the Young*. New York: McGraw-Hill, 1974.

Modern Maturity Magazine, American Association of Retired People, Long Beach, California (any issue).

OBJECTIVE: To explore attitudes and stereotypes about aging in America.

ACTIVITY

Analyze TV commercials, looking at the relationship of the product advertised and the person in the commercial. What conclusions can be drawn relating persons and products to stereotyped notions about youth and age? Is advanced age ever portrayed as a desirable time of life? Collect examples from magazines and other media.

STUDENT RESOURCES

All media channels in the culture.

READING

Butler, Robert, *Why Survive? Being Old in America.* New York: Harper & Row, 1975.

Comfort, Alex, *A Good Age.* New York: Crown, 1976.

Curtin, Sharon, *Nobody Ever Died of Old Age.* Boston: Little, Brown, 1973.

GOAL TWO: To help the student affectively deal with the idea of personal death and the deaths of significant others.

OBJECTIVE: To explore the students' own feelings about the aged and getting old.

ACTIVITIES

1. The purpose of this activity is to help the students understand some of the physical limitations of the aged. Select students to do any or all of the following:

   a. Put cotton in ears.

   b. Crumple aluminum foil and put it in shoes.

   c. Wear very smudged eyeglasses.

   d. Tape tennis balls on the inside of each kneecap.

   e. Tie lollipop sticks to fingers.

   Have impaired students interact with other students and attempt normal activity. Discuss what happens.

2. View and discuss films on aging.

STUDENT RESOURCES

OTHER MEDIA

Aging (motion picture; 30 minutes, color). Two old men discuss their attitudes about getting old. Available from

Audio-Visual Center, Indiana University, Bloomington, Ind. 47401.

To Be Growing Older (motion picture; 13 minutes, color). Young people and old people give views on being old. Available from Billy Budd Films, 235 E. 57th Street, New York, N.Y. 10022.

I Think (motion picture). White Plains, N.Y.: Wombat Productions. The film shows the difficulties young persons face as they struggle to develop identities despite pressure to conform; young girl weighs relationship with older woman. Available from Mass Media Associates, 2116 N. Charles St., Baltimore, Md. 21218.

TEACHER RESOURCES

See other resources on aging for this grade.

GOAL THREE: To make the student an informed consumer of medical and funeral services.

OBJECTIVES: To discover the medical context of dying in modern America and to introduce the student to the technology, professional duties, and attitudes surrounding death.

ACTIVITIES

1. Have students describe death as it is presented on television, including news, medical, police, and drama shows. Discuss whether this matches the student's own experiences.

2. Have class members make a list of characteristics of TV death scenes for future comparison with more factual data.

3. Student learns about the role of the modern hospital in the dying process. Physician or nurse talks about:

a. life-prolonging measures in a hospital

b. daily hospital routine

4. Investigate the concept of a hospice.

STUDENT RESOURCES

READING

Annas, George, *The Rights of Hospital Patients: The Basic ACLU Guide to a Hospital Patient's Rights*. New York: Avon Books, 1975.

Rubin, Theodore, *Emergency Room Diary*. New York: Grosset & Dunlap, 1972. How physicians respond in critical situations.

Saunders, Cicely, "St. Christopher's Hospice," in *Death: Current Perspectives*, ed. Edwin Shneidman. Palo Alto, Calif.: Mayfield Publishing, 1976.

OTHER MEDIA

"Walk in the World For Me" (filmstrip) in *Death and Dying: Closing the Circle (Part III)*. Pleasantville, N.Y.: Guidance Associates, 1977. Dying of seventeen-year-old from leukemia as told by his mother; includes discussion of good hospital care. Lund, Doris, *Eric*. Philadelphia: Lippincott, 1974. Same story as filmstrip.

Future Unknown (motion picture; 15 minutes, B/W). Pittsburgh, Pa.: University of Pittsburgh, n.d. Young female cancer patient finds a friend in the midst of an impersonal hospital setting.

Dignity of Death (motion picture; 30 minutes, color). New York: ABC News, n.d. Story of St. Christopher's Hospice and its staff's humane treatment of the dying. Available at 7 W. 66th St., New York, N.Y. 10023.

TEACHER RESOURCES

READING

Buckingham, Robert, Joan Kron, and Donna Bettes, *The Hospice Concept*. New York: Highly Specialized Promotions, 1977. Available from Highly Specialized Promotions, P.O. Box 989 GPO, Brooklyn, N.Y. 11202.

Kastenbaum, Robert, and Ruth Aisenberg, *The Psychology of Death*. New York: Springer, 1972. An early encyclopedic work about death that covers almost every facet of the subject. See especially Chapters 9 and 15 for this goal.

LaSagna, Louis, "The Physician's Behavior Towards the Dying Patient," in *The Dying Patient*, ed. Orville Brim and others. New York: Russell Sage Foundation, 1970.

Mauksch, Hans, "The Organizational Context of Dying," in *Death: The Final Stage of Growth*, ed. Elisabeth Kübler-Ross. Englewood Cliffs, N.J.: Prentice-Hall, 1975.

Neale, Robert, "Between the Nipple and the Everlasting Arms," in *Death and Society*, eds. James P. Carse and Arlene B. Dallery. New York: Harcourt Brace Jovanovich, 1977.

Patient Care, Vol. 11, No. 12, June 15, 1977. Special Issue: "When Caring Is All That's Left to Give."

Saunders, Cicely, "St. Christopher's Hospice," in *Death: Current Perspectives*, ed. Edwin Shneidman. Palo Alto, Calif.: Mayfield Publishing Co., 1976.

Stoddard, Sandal, *The Hospice Movement: A Better Way to Care for the Dying*. New York: Stein and Day, 1977.

GOAL FOUR: To help the student formulate socioethical issues related to death and define value judgments these issues raise.

OBJECTIVE: To introduce the students to basic ethical and social policy issues connected with death and dying.

ACTIVITIES

1. Isolate issues of interest to teacher and class (e.g., death with dignity, euthanasia, suicide, transplants, capital punishment, body disposal, and ecology). These are topics suitable for formal debate, research, and written reports. Classroom can become a courtroom with mock or real cases tried before juries. Have students write to Euthanasia Educational Council and the Society for the Right to Die for information and free pamphlets before debates or written reports.
2. Invite a local elected official to class to discuss political views on these issues.

STUDENT RESOURCES

READING
Bender, David, ed., *Problem of Death: Opposing Viewpoints.* Anoka, Minn.: Greenhaven Press, 1975. Use point–counterpoint format to discuss ethical issues and social practice—stimulates class discussion and individual critical thinking. Available from Box 831, Anoka, Minn. 55303.

Langone, John, *Death Is a Noun: A View of the End of Life.* Boston: Little, Brown, 1972. Issues of ethics and social policy such as euthanasia, suicide; encourages students to make own judgments.

Euthanasia Educational Council, 250 W. 57th St., New York, N.Y. 10019. Many handout materials on euthanasia.

Society for the Right to Die, 250 West 57th St., New York, N.Y. 10019. Legislative handbook and other materials.

OTHER MEDIA

Death of a Peasant (motion picture). Young man in World War II flees Nazis and and decides to kill himself rather than face probable torture. Available from Mass Media, 1720 Chouteau, St. Louis, Mo. 63103. Same story with different point of view is a movie called *Joseph Schutz* from Wombat Productions, 77 Tarrytown Rd., White Plains, N.Y. 10607.

Last and Lasting Gift (motion picture; 28 minutes). Excellent film on organ donation. Available free from Inland Empire Resource Center, 2 W. Olive, Redlands, Calif. 92373.

Medicine, Morality, and the Law: Euthanasia (motion picture; 30 minutes, B/W). Three case studies with different points of view. Available from University of Michigan TV Center, 910 Maynard St., Ann Arbor, Mich. 49619.

The Mercy-Killers (motion picture; 30 minutes, B/W). Frank discussion of euthanasia using actual cases. Available from Time-Life Films, 43 W. 16th St., New York, N.Y. 10011.

Right to Die (motion picture; 56 minutes, color). Excellent film interviews of dying patients; raises questions of death with dignity, active and passive euthanasia. Available from Macmillan Films, MacQuesten Pkwy. South, Mt. Vernon, N.Y. 10550.

TEACHER RESOURCES

READING

Carse, James, and Arlene Dallery, eds., *Death and Society*. New York: Harcourt Brace Jovanovich, 1977. Anthology includes many important issues: body donation, abortion, capital punishment, euthanasia, and so on.

Kastenbaum, Robert, and Ruth Aisenberg, *The Psychology of Death*. New York: Springer, 1972. Chapters 9 through 16.

Maguire, Daniel, *Death by Choice*. New York: Schocken Books, 1973. Good discussion of ethical and legal issues surrounding euthanasia.

Veatch, Robert, *Death, Dying and the Biological Revolution*. New Haven, Conn.: Yale University Press, 1976. Discussion by an outstanding ethicist on the problems of death and dying. Often technical but very worthwhile reading.

GRADES: 10, 11

GOAL ONE: To inform the students of facts not currently widespread in the culture.

OBJECTIVES: To acquaint the student with current legal and medical definitions of death and to introduce the problematic character of those definitions.

ACTIVITIES

1. Learn the rationale for and practical application of the Harvard Criteria for Brain Death (see appendix).
2. Learn earlier definitions of death.
3. Discuss state and local legislative activity on brain death, transplants, and right-to-die legislation.

STUDENT RESOURCES

READING
(See resources in grades 8 and 9 as well.)

Black, Henry Campbell, *Black's Law Dictionary* (4th ed.). St. Paul, Minn.: West Publishing Co., 1968. Look up definitions of death.

Society for the Right to Die Legislative Handbook (pamphlet). Available from the Society for the Right to Die, 250 W. 57th St., New York, N.Y. 10019.

An Essay on the Problems Related to the Prolongation of Life by Technological Methods (pamphlet). Available from the Unit on Church and Society, 475 Riverside Drive, RM 1244K, New York, N.Y. 10027. Copies for class available; excellent discussion of ethical problems.

TEACHER RESOURCES

READING
Veatch, Robert, *Death, Dying and the Biological Revolution.* New Haven, Conn.: Yale University Press, 1976.

OBJECTIVE: To acquaint student with the legalities and problems of body and organ donation.

ACTIVITIES

1. Invite local physician to discuss current hospital practices for body and organ donation as well as physician's experience with families.
2. Ask representative of eye bank, kidney organization, or the like to speak.

STUDENT AND TEACHER RESOURCES

READING
Morgan, Ernest, *Manual for Simple Burial and Death Education.* Burnsville, N.C.: Celo Press, 1977. How and where to

donate body parts. Order from Alternatives, 701 No. Eugene St., Greensboro, N.C. 27401.

OTHER MEDIA

Last and Lasting Gift (motion picture; 28 minutes). How organs are donated and used. Available from Inland Empire, Human Resources Center, 2 W. Olive, Redlands, Calif. 92373.

Copy of Uniform Anatomical Gift Act (see appendix).

GOAL TWO: To help the student affectively deal with the idea of personal death and the deaths of significant others.

OBJECTIVE: To make the students aware of their responses to loss and ways of coping with that loss.

ACTIVITIES

1. Students write autobiographical accounts of their own grief situations; this does not have to be shared with other class members if the student does not choose to do so.
2. Class visits by school counselor or clergy to talk about how they perceive and handle grief as professionals.
3. See and discuss films and filmstrips on how others handle and define grief.

STUDENT RESOURCES

READING

Beckman, Gunnel, *Admission to the Feast.* New York: Holt, Rinehart & Winston, 1971. Fiction—letter of nineteen-year-old dying girl to her friend.

Bernstein, Joanne, *Loss and How to Cope with It.* New York:

Seabury Books, 1977. Very suitable for adolescents as well as adults.

Irish, Jerry, *A Boy Thirteen: Reflections on Death*. Philadelphia: Westminster Press, 1975.

OTHER MEDIA

All the Way Home (motion picture; 103 minutes, B/W). Young boy and his mother try to cope with the death of the father. Excellent portrait of many family members. Available from Films Incorporated, 1144 Wilmette Ave., Wilmette, Ill. 60091. Based on the novel by James Agee, *A Death in the Family*. New York: Avon Books, 1959.

"Loss," "The Grief Process," and "When Someone Is Grieving" (filmstrips) in *Loss and Grief*. Costa Mesa, Calif.: Concept Media, 1977. Good didactic teaching about the feelings associated with loss and grief. Available from 1500 Adams Ave., Costa Mesa, Calif. 92626.

How Could I Not Be Among You (motion picture; 28 minutes, color). Young poet confronts his own death from leukemia. Available from Highly Specialized Promotions, P.O. Box 989 GPO, Brooklyn, N.Y. 11202. Ted Rosenthal's poetry can also be found in the last chapter in *Death: Current Perspectives*, ed. Edwin Shneidman. Palo Alto, Calif.: Mayfield Publishing, 1976.

"Walk in the World for Me" (filmstrip) in *Death and Dying: Closing the Circle, Part III*. Pleasantville, N.Y.: Guidance Associates, 1975. Mother's grief over her dying seventeen-year-old son.

TEACHER RESOURCES

READING

The School Counselor, Vol. 24, No. 5, May 1977. Special issue on death education.

Hodge, James, "They That Mourn" in *Journal of Religion and Health*, Vol. 11, No. 3, July 1972. Outlines grief process in detail.

Schoenberg, Bernard, and others, *Bereavement*. New York: Columbia University Press, 1975.

————, *Loss and Grief*. New York: Columbia University Press, 1970.

GOAL THREE: To make the student an informed consumer of medical and funeral services.

OBJECTIVE: To acquaint students with the financial aspects of medical care for terminal illness and life-threatening situations.

ACTIVITIES

1. Have class collect information in order to prepare questions to ask health-care representatives. Teacher guides discussion so class can be aware of issues of socialized medicine, government proposals, pending legislation, and so forth.

2. Invite persons concerned with the business aspects of the health-care industry to discuss the costs of health care (e.g., nursing home administrator, hospital administrator, hospital social worker, health insurance representative, political representatives).

3. Call or visit the local hospital to find out costs for room, use of surgical equipment, blood, anesthesia, and the like.

4. Have students prepare hospital or nursing home billing for hypothetical patient for a minimum two-week stay.

STUDENT AND
TEACHER RESOURCES

READING

Life and Death and Medicine. San Francisco: W. H. Freeman, 1973. Chapters 4, 9, 10, 11, 12, and 13. Originally a special issue of *Scientific American.*

Steinfels, Peter, and Robert Veatch, eds., *Death Inside Out.* New York: Harper Forum Books, 1975. Chapter 3.

OBJECTIVE: To have students explore decisions about death and dying as these decisions would affect them and their families.

ACTIVITY

Students discuss with their families their wishes and possible decisions concerning euthanasia, organ donation, heroic measures, and so on. Return to class with information and/or discuss their own wishes in these matters. Note: The factual information on these issues has been covered in grades 8 and 9 (Goal 1) and 10 and 11 (Goal 1).

TEACHER RESOURCES

(See other resources in grades 8 and 9 [Goal 1] and 10 and 11 [Goal 1].)

READING

Behnke, John, and Sissela Bok, eds., *The Dilemmas of Euthanasia.* New York: Anchor Press, 1975.

Steinfels, Peter, and Robert Veatch, eds., *Death Inside Out.* New York: Harper Forum Book, 1975. Chapters 3 and 4.

GOAL THREE: To make the student an informed consumer of medical and funeral services.

OBJECTIVE: To introduce the student to a variety of methods of body disposal, current funeral practices, and relative costs.

ACTIVITIES

1. Visit funeral home to find out services and costs. Call or visit crematory, cemetery, mausoleum, and columbarium to find out their costs.
2. Make list of all available means of body disposal and comparative costs.
3. Have students talk to family member who tends to make funeral arrangements about average costs and general family patterns regarding funeral arrangements and body disposal.
4. Ask local planned funeral or memorial society representative to talk to class or send literature.

STUDENT RESOURCES

READING

Morgan, Ernest, *Manual for Death Education and Simple Burial.* Burnsville, N.C.: Celo Press, 1977. Order from Alternatives, 107 N. Eugene St., Greensboro, N.C. 27401.

Casket and Sunnyside, funeral trade magazine; get copies from local funeral directors.

OTHER MEDIA

The Great American Funeral (motion picture). Close look at the funeral industry and all its services and costs (may be outdated) with commentary by Jessica Mitford. Available from Mass Media, 1720 Chouteau Ave., St. Louis, Mo. 63103.

"A Time To Mourn—A Time To Choose" (filmstrip) in *Death and Dying: Closing the Circle, Part II.* Pleasantville, N.Y.: Guidance Associates, 1975.

TEACHER RESOURCES

READING

Blackwell, Robert, and Wayne Talaryk, *American Attitudes Toward Death and Funerals.* Evanston, Ill.: Casket Manufacturers Association, 1972. Trade report and statistics.

Federal Trade Commission Report on Funeral Practices. Washington, D.C.: U.S. Govt. Bureau of Consumer Protection, 1975.

Habenstein, Robert, and William Lamers, *History of American Funeral Directing.* Milwaukee, Wis.: Bulfin Printers, 1962.

GOAL FOUR: To help the student formulate socioethical issues related to death and define value judgments these issues raise.

OBJECTIVE: To acquaint the student with the legal and moral issues reflected in the problems of the prolongation of life and the termination of life.

ACTIVITIES

1. Study the Living Will and the Patient's Bill of Rights as well as the American Civil Liberties Union handbook, *The Rights of Hospital Patients.* Compare the

ALCU Model Patient's Bill of Rights to the AHA Patient's Bill of Rights (see appendix).

2. Debate issues that the class selects as the most important moral and legal issues concerning death.

3. Discuss the differences in various state statutes on the "right to die," using the *Legislative Handbook* of the Society for the Right to Die.

STUDENT AND TEACHER RESOURCES

READING

American Friends Service Committee, *Who Shall Live: Man's Control over Birth and Death*. New York: Hill & Wang, 1970.

Behnke, John, and Sissela Bok, eds., *The Dilemmas of Euthanasia*. New York: Anchor Press, 1975.

Bender, David, *Problems of Death: Opposing Viewpoints*. Anoka, Minn.: Green Haven Press, 1974.

OTHER MEDIA

Logan's Run (motion picture). Futuristic society ends life at 35. Send for movie catalog from Films Inc., 1144 Wilmette Ave., Wilmette, Ill. 60091, to find out whether this movie and *Soylent Green* are available, and their rental price.

Soylent Green (motion picture). Planned death in futuristic society according to last wishes (see *Logan's Run* source).

Medicine, Morality, and the Law: Euthanasia (motion picture; 30 minutes, B/W), Available from the University of Michigan TV Center, 910 Maynard, Ann Arbor, Mich. 49619.

The Right to Die (motion picture; 56 minutes, color). Available from MacMillan Films, 34 MacQuesten Pkwy. South, Mt. Vernon, N.Y. 10550.

Whose Life Is It Anyway? (motion picture; 53 minutes, color). Young disabled man chooses to die; physicians fight for life at any cost. Available from Eccentric Circle Workshop, P.O. Box 1481, Evanston, Ill. 60204.

Copy of a Living Will from Euthanasia Education Council, 250 West 57th St., New York, N.Y. 10019 (see appendix).

Legislative Handbook from the Society for the Right to Die, 250 West 57th Street, New York, N.Y. 10019.

American Hospital Association Patient's Bill of Rights and American Civil Liberties Union Model Patient's Bill of Rights (see appendix). For extra copies of American Hospital Association Patient's Bill of Rights, write to the American Hospital Association, 840 N. Lake Shore Drive, Chicago, Ill. 60610.

GRADE: 12

GOAL ONE: To inform the students of facts not currently widespread in the culture.

OBJECTIVE: To survey theories about suicide and its occurrence in our culture.

GOAL TWO: To help the student affectively deal with the idea of personal death and the deaths of significant others.

OBJECTIVE: To have the students explore their own feelings about suicide.

ACTIVITIES

1. Isolate suicide themes in the lyrics of current popular music and poetry.

   a. What is the relationship of the suicidal thoughts
      and gestures in the song to the theme of the song?

   b. Is there a relationship between the artist's life and
      suicidal thoughts?

2. Read about the lives of well-known persons who
   have committed suicide (Marilyn Monroe, Ernest
   Hemingway, Freddie Prinz, Sylvia Plath, Anne Sexton).

3. Identify famous suicides in history and literature and
   their reasons for suicide.

4. Role play trying to talk someone out of jumping off a
   ledge on the eighty-first floor.

5. Talk about why adolescents commit suicide. Teacher
   should provide empirical data as to why teens commit suicide and what counseling services especially
   for teens are available in the community. This discussion must be conducted in an open, empathic setting
   with confidentiality understood within the classroom.

6. Read and write poetry about suicide; see especially
   poems of John Berryman, Sylvia Plath, and Anne
   Sexton.

STUDENT AND
TEACHER RESOURCES

READING

Alvarez, A., *The Savage God*. New York: Bantam Books,
1972. Most comprehensive study of suicide from literary
and historical point of view. Includes insight into Sylvia
Plath's death and author's own attempted suicide.

Grollman, Earl, *Suicide*. Boston: Beacon Press, 1971. Best short summary of the topic.

Haim, Andre, *Adolescent Suicide*. New York: International University Press, 1974.

Kastenbaum, Robert, and Ruth Aisenberg, *The Psychology of Death*. New York: Springer, 1972. Chapters 11, 12, 13, and 14.

Klagsbrun, Francine, *Youth and Suicide: Too Young to Die*. Boston: Houghton Mifflin, 1976.

Plath, Sylvia, *Ariel*. New York: Harper & Row, 1966.

————, *The Bell Jar*. New York: Harper & Row, 1971.

Sexton, Anne, *The Awful Rowing Toward God*. Boston: Houghton Mifflin, 1975.

————, *The Death Notebooks* (2nd ed.). Boston: Houghton Mifflin, 1974.

OTHER MEDIA

The Threat of Suicide (videorecording; 27 minutes, color). New York: Network for Continuing Medical Education, n.d. For health-care professionals to sensitize them to potential suicides. Available from Network for Continuing Medical Education, Columbus Circle, New York, N.Y. 10023.

"Adolescent Suicide" (audiorecording) in *Death, Grief and Bereavement Series*. Available from The Center for Death Education and Research, University of Minnesota, Minneapolis, Minn. 55414.

Songs: "Ode to Billy Joe," Bobby Gentry; "Save the Life of My Child," Paul Simon; "Vincent," Don McLean; and others.

A Case of Suicide (motion picture; 30 minutes, B/W). Case

history and reactions to a young woman's suicide. Available from Time-Life Films, 43 W. 16th St., New York, N.Y. 10001.

Rick: An Adolescent Suicide (motion picture; 30 minutes, B/W). Psychological reconstruction of a seventeen-year-old's suicide. Available from Medical Media Network, 10995 LeConte Ave., Los Angeles, Calif. 90024.

Romeo and Juliet (motion picture). Classic story of young love and death. Available from Films, Inc., 1144 Wilmette Ave., Wilmette, Ill. 60091.

GOAL TWO: To help the student affectively deal with the idea of personal death and the deaths of significant others.

OBJECTIVE: To acquaint the student with experiences connected with the crises of death and dying that may not fit into commonly accepted reality.

ACTIVITIES

1. Students should be encouraged to write about (or may share in class) experiences connected with death and dying that still puzzle them because they seem to have no rational or acceptable explanations. These are experiences that include visions, postdeath contacts of any kind, or mystical experiences that may border on the occult. (Note to the teacher: About one-third of the class usually have had such experiences, but some may be reluctant to discuss them and should not be pushed.)

2. Have students research reports of unusual phenomena connected with death and dying, and

discuss the adequacy of the research methods used as well as the content of the findings.

Questions such as:

a. Did the researcher influence findings by the way questions were phrased?

b. Did the research begin with a basic untested belief?

c. Do the data justify the conclusions?

3. Discuss concepts of mortality and immortality as found in students' families and community.

STUDENT RESOURCES

READING

Bach, Richard, *Jonathan Livingston Seagull*. New York: Macmillan, 1970.

Monroe, Robert, *Journeys Out of the Body*. Garden City, N.Y.: Anchor Press, 1973.

Moody, Raymond, *Life After Life*. New York: Bantam Books, 1976.

————, *Reflections on Life After Life*. New York: Bantam Books, 1977. Case histories of people with similar experiences connected with dying and trauma, leading one to the conclusion that there is "something more" that is not yet known about the experience of dying.

Olander, Joseph, and Martin Harry Greenberg, *Time of Passage*. New York: Taplinger Publishing Company, 1978. Science fiction stories about death and dying.

Osis, Karlis, and Erlendur Haroldsson, *At the Hour of Death*. New York: Avon Books, 1977.

Saint–Exupéry, Antoine de, *The Little Prince*. New York: Harcourt Brace, 1943.

TEACHER RESOURCES

READING

Grof, Stanislav, and Joan Halifax, *The Human Encounter with Death*. New York: Dutton, 1977. Description of LSD-assisted therapy for the terminally ill.

Kalish, Richard, and David Reynolds, *Death and Ethnicity: A Psychocultural Study*. Los Angeles, Calif.: University of Southern California Press, 1976.

OBJECTIVE: To help students develop a meaningful philosophy of life and death.

ACTIVITIES

1. Find out the purpose of eulogies by writing a eulogy on:

   a. What others will say about you.

   b. What you would say about yourself.

2. Class discussion on what death means to each student. Can be stimulated by writing of essays, poetry, fiction; use of music, art, inspirational readings, and so forth.

3. Investigation by student of personal religious traditions concerning death and dying. If no religious traditions are present, student can investigate family's personal philosophy of life and death. Try out experiential exercises in *Manual of Death Education and Simple Burial* and *Personal Death Awareness*.

READING

Ball, Geraldine, *Innerchange, A Journey into Self-Learning Through Group Interaction.* La Mesa, Calif.: Human Development Training Institute, 1977. Specify Unit 32, "Life and Death," for the senior high school level. Provides worksheets, discussion cards, resources, and so on for feelings about death with coordinated art and music appreciation activities. Available from Human Development Training Institute, Inc., 7574 University Ave., La Mesa, Calif. 92041 or call toll free (800) 854-2166.

Bible. Read Ecclesiastes for discussion of individual death and the meaning of life; Ezekiel 37 for resurrection of the physical body; I Corinthians 15 for resurrection of the spiritual body; Psalm 23 for consolation in the face of death.

Feifel, Herman, ed., *The Meaning of Death.* New York: McGraw-Hill, 1959. Part I, "Theoretical Outlooks on Death," applies to the discussion here.

Gordon, Audrey, "The Jewish View of Death: Guidelines for Mourning" in *Death: The Final Stage of Growth,* ed. Elisabeth Kübler–Ross. Englewood Cliffs, N.J.: Prentice-Hall, 1975.

Gordon, David, *Overcoming the Fear of Death.* New York: Macmillan, 1970.

Grollman, Earl, *Concerning Death.* Boston: Beacon Press, 1974. Chapters 5, 6, and 7 concern Catholic, Protestant, and Jewish traditions.

Klein, Norma, *Sunshine.* New York: Avon Books, 1974.

Kübler–Ross, Elisabeth, *On Death and Dying.* New York:

Macmillan, 1969. Stage theory of dying; classic work in the field.

Neale, Robert, *The Art of Dying*. New York: Harper & Row, 1973. Exercises as way of preparing students for own death.

Wilcox, Sandra, and Marilyn Sutton, *Understanding Death and Dying: An Interdisciplinary Approach*. Port Washington, N.Y.: Alfred Publishing Co., 1978. See Part One: "The Definition and Meaning of Death," and Part Two: "The Experience of Dying" especially. Has structured exercises and literary selections the teacher will find useful for the students.

Worden, J. W., and W. Procter, *Personal Death Awareness*. Englewood Cliffs, N.J.: Prentice-Hall, 1976. Has many exercises the teacher can choose for class activities.

OTHER MEDIA

"The Meaning of Death" (filmstrip) in *Death and Dying: Closing the Circle, Part I*. Pleasantville, N.Y.: Guidance Associates, 1975. Psychologist Robert Lifton talks about death, the meaning of life, and immortality.

The Mark Waters Story (videorecording; 29 minutes, color). True story of dying newspaperman who writes his own obituary. Available from Public Television Library, 475 L'Enfant Plaza S.W., Washington, D.C. 20024.

Between the Cup and the Lip (motion picture; 11 minutes, color). Symbolic animated film of the inevitability of death. Available from Mass Media, 1720 Chouteau, St. Louis, Mo. 63103.

Death (motion picture; 43 minutes, B/W). Powerful film showing actual death, body wrapping, and common hospital treatment of the dying. Available from Filmmakers Library, 290 West End Ave., New York, N.Y. 10001.

The Lyn Helton Story (motion picture; 10 minutes, color). Diary of innermost thoughts and feelings of young woman dying of cancer. Available from American Medical Association Film Library, 535 N. Dearborn, Chicago, Ill. 60610.

Soon There Will Be No More of Me (motion picture; 10 minutes, B/W). Young mother dying shows feelings of fear and concern for her children. Available from Churchill Films, 662 N. Robertson Blvd., Los Angeles, Calif. 90069.

You See I've Had a Life (motion picture; 30 minutes, B/W). Dying teenager and her family share their experiences. Quality rather than length of life is stressed. Available from Eccentric Circle Cinema Workshop, Box 1481, Evanston, Ill. 60204.

Songs: "And When I Die," Blood Sweat and Tears; "Home," Procul Harum; "The Art of Dying," George Harrison; "Tapestry," Carole King; "Morning Side" (for my children), Neil Diamond; many others.

GOAL THREE: To make the student an informed consumer of medical and funeral services.

OBJECTIVE: To acquaint students with insurance and wills.

ACTIVITIES

1. Invite a lawyer to speak on wills and probate.
2. Draft a will.
3. Have insurance representatives in class to talk about various kinds of life and health insurance.

READING

Annas, George, *The Rights of Hospital Patients: The Basic ACLU Guide to a Hospital Patients Rights*. New York: Avon Books, 1975. Chapter 16.

Considine, Mille, and Ruth Pool, *Wills: A Dead Giveaway*. New York: Doubleday, 1974. Some humorous, some serious, but an interesting collection of differing wills.

OTHER MEDIA

Estate Planning (motion picture; 8 minutes, color). Ames, Iowa: University of Iowa, 1973. Covers estates and estate taxes.

FURTHER READING

ALLYN, MILDRED V., comp., *About Aging: A Catalog of Films* (3rd ed.). Los Angeles: University of Southern California Press, 1977.

BERG, DAVID W., and GEORGE G. DAUGHERTY, comp., *Death Education: Audio Visual Source Book*. De Kalb, Ill.: Educational Perspectives Associates, 1976.

BERNSTEIN, JOANNE, *Books to Help Children Cope with Separation and Loss*. New York: R. R. Bowker Company, 1977.

COOK, SARAH SHEETS, and others, *Children and Dying: An Exploration and Selective Bibliographies*. New York: Health Sciences Publishing Company, 1974.

DUKE, PHYLLIS, "Media on Death and Dying," *Omega*, 6, No. 3 (1975), 275–287.

FASSLER, JOAN, *Helping Children Cope*. New York: The Free Press, 1978.

Forum for Death Education and Counseling Newsletter, available from Forum for Death Education and Counseling, P.O. Box 1226, Arlington, Virginia 22210.

FULTON, ROBERT, comp., *A Bibliography on Death, Grief and Bereavement 1845–1975*. New York: Arno Press, 1975.

LEVITON, DANIEL, "Death Education," in *New Meanings of Death*, ed. Herman Feifel. New York: McGraw-Hill, 1977.

We think of ourselves as consumers when we go to the supermarket or find a defect in our new car; but we do not usually think of ourselves as consumers when we go to the hospital, the physician's office, or when we make funeral arrangements for someone who has died. Yet we can pay a significant amount of money to physicians and hospitals, and a funeral can cost as much as a car.

If we are to get the most for our money and the best service we can afford, we need to think of ourselves as consumers of goods and services in our relationship with the health and funeral industries. If we are to help our children become wise consumers of medical and funeral

Consumer Information for Medical and Funeral Services

Chapter **8**

services, we must have the proper preparation and information to share with them. This chapter is concerned with the physician–patient relationship, the hospital–patient relationship, and the business relationship between the funeral director and the purchaser of funeral services. There are legal and ethical dimensions to these relationships. Consumer recognition of these dimensions will enhance both the services rendered and the human interactions that ensue.

THE HEALTH INDUSTRY

One of the most important parts of the physician–patient relationship is in the area of decision making. Who has the power to make the final decision concerning the best interests of the patient? Is it the patient him- or herself? The family? The physician? Public policy? Health insurance companies? Institutions caring for the patient? The question itself demonstrates the need for a clearer understanding of the physician–patient relationship; the answers indicate that there is no definitive norm by which to answer the question. All the foregoing answers could be correct, depending upon a particular situation. It seems to us that it is the patient who has a right to decide about his or her own care, because it is the person who will be most affected by the decisions made. This means that we must get the fullest possible information from the physician in order to make an informed decision, and having learned all we can, the decisions for our health and life are ultimately ours. At the moment, this right to decide for ourselves is not clearly defined in the law and is considered on an ad hoc basis as the need arises. This right to decide affects the right to die (euthanasia), the right to be free of pain, the right to refuse medical treatment, the right to institutional care for the dying or the right to die at home, and to know the diagnosis and prognosis of disease.

At present, the rights of patients in relationship to their physicians or hospitals are not very clear. The American Civil Liberties Union's book *The Rights of Hospital Patients* claims that there is no clear-cut right to health care in the United States except for treatment in emergency medical situations. So the most efficient way to protect ourselves in a medical relationship is to be confident of the person with whom we have that relationship—the physician. Before engaging the services of a primary-care physician, we should be confident that we are being responsible in our choice if the physician answers the following questions to our satisfaction:

1. Do you have a medical specialty (internal medicine, obstetrics and gynecology, orthopedics, psychiatry, family practice, cardiology, and so forth)?

2. Are you board certified?

3. With what hospitals do you affiliate?

4. Do you have any teaching duties or special research interests at the hospital?

5. Do you believe your patients have a right to a complete and honest diagnosis and prognosis at all times?

6. Under what circumstances, if any, would you not disclose information?

7. Under what circumstances, if any, would you heed family wishes instead of the wishes of your patient?

8. Would you honor your dying patient's wish to die pain free with

dignity, even if your state had not yet adopted right-to-die legislation?

9. How would final decisions on medical care be made—in consultation with the patient? by the patient alone? by yourself alone? in consultation with other physicians?

10. Would you object to second and third medical opinions the patient might wish while in your care?

11. Do you have a financial interest in any clinic, pharmacy, or physicians' group that might limit your patients' freedom of choice?

12. Do you have a financial interest in any for-profit hospital or health-care institution?

13. What do you consider to be an optimum physician–patient relationship?

14. What are your fees?

15. Can you be contacted by telephone outside of office hours?

16. Who takes care of your patients when you are not available?

How these questions are answered should tell us whether we want this person as our physician or not. Other things we might want to check mentally while we are talking with the physician are:

1. Is the physician making an effort to make me feel comfortable?

2. Do I feel as if I have his or her full attention and time?

3. Is this a person I feel I could get along with?

4. Is the waiting room organized in an orderly fashion, or do the people waiting seem disgruntled?

5. Was my appointment kept within a reasonable amount of time (thirty minutes)?

6. Was I treated with courtesy and dignity by the office personnel and nurses as well as the physician?

7. Was it initially difficult to make this appointment with the physician's office?

We recognize that not all physicians have the time for interview sessions before an appointment is made for a physical exam. Some physicians might be willing to answer some questions on the phone. All physicians should be willing to answer these questions at the first appointment for a physical examination. The answers to questions 1 through 4 (page 212) can be found under the physician's name in the Directory of Medical Specialists published by Marquis Publishing. This listing also provides other personal information about the physician such as schooling, age, birthplace, and so on.

Choosing the right physician is often a trial-and-error procedure, sometimes taking months and years. The most important element often lacking in a good medical relationship is truth. We must ask if we are truthful with the physician, and is he or she truthful with us? We cannot expect our medical helpers to be clairvoyant about our feelings of illness nor omnipotent in their ability to cure. We can act on the implied agreement that the physician is working in our best interests and that we will responsibly follow advice and treatment suggestions after the physician has made full disclosure of medical facts. If the breakdown in trust and communication between us and our physician is so complete as to be irreparable, then we must look elsewhere. A reasoned, constructive letter informing the physician why this change is necessary can help physicians to improve their services to us.

Since this is a book on death education, our focus is on the relationship between the terminally ill patient, the hospital, and the physician. *The Rights of Hospital Patients*, a handbook published by the American Civil Liberties Union, notes:

When a patient is categorized as terminal, he is often simultaneously deprived of both his right to know the truth and his right to consent to treatment and to exercise discretion in choosing a place and time to die. Between 70 and 80 percent of all Americans now die in hospitals or nursing homes, making the problems of the terminally ill in these institutions extremely important. Doctors frequently define the terminally ill patient as "one I can't do anything for," and often use this as a justification for depriving the patient of what the doctor would otherwise consider basic human rights. [P. 162]

Studies of patients who are diagnosed as having a terminal illness indicate that 90 percent of them want to know their diagnosis and are relieved when they are told their condition straightforwardly. Research among physicians indicates that between 60 and 90 percent of all physicians prefer to withhold a diagnosis of terminal illness from their patients, using the rationales that "the patient knows anyway" or that their responsibility has been discharged if the family has been informed and they can tell the patient if they wish.

The patient may wish to keep the news of terminal illness confidential between him- or herself and the physician, but the physician may feel compelled to inform the family against the patient's wishes. In this case the patient has the legal right to insist on confidentiality, and disclosure of medical information may not be made without the patient's consent. There is a question as to whether a patient has given informed consent if not told complete medical information and diagnosis about a fatal illness. Without informed consent, the patient's permission for the physician and the hospital to perform surgical and medical procedures is invalid. When the final phase of fatal illness occurs, it is especially important for the patient to know

whether or not the hospital or physician has left verbal or
signed orders concerning the cardiac resuscitation of that
patient in the event of heart failure. The physician should
confer with the patient concerning the patient's wishes,
inform the patient of the proposed course of action, and
sign the medical order should a policy of no-resuscitation
be agreed upon.

Most people fear suffering more than dying itself.
Medication for pain relief is not a legal right, although it
can be administered in sufficient dosages to relieve pain
(and possibly hasten the death) if the physician agrees.
Only if the patient insists upon his or her human rights to
a dignified pain-free death will hospital rules and physicians' orders change to reflect public wishes in this regard.
As the ACLU handbook says:

> When he was dying of cancer, columnist Stewart Alsop wrote
> eloquently of the experience and suggested that the patients be
> allowed "to decide for themselves how much pain-killing drug
> they will take—it is, after all, they, not the doctors, who are
> suffering the agonies." This "right" is another example of a polit-
> ical right that patients can only translate into a legal right or
> institutional policy by exerting political pressure. [P. 166]

Hospital admission policies do not always guarantee a
bed for the dying patient. Some utilization review boards
of hospitals have established the policy that beds for the
last phase of hopeless illness will be made available only if
there are sufficient beds to meet all other medical needs.
Harsh as this may appear, it reflects the concern of hospital management that the hospital not become a dumping
ground for dying persons when further medical treatment
is not possible. The hospice movement and greater education of the public can help to show that some dying people
want to be treated and allowed to die at home or possibly

in a hospice facility. Dying at home not only requires the willingness of the family to meet the needs of the patient but also the cooperation of the medical profession as well, since it is the physician who must manage the pain-control program and other medical problems the dying patient may face. A hospice can be a place for the last weeks of dying, featuring a specially trained staff for psychological support, control of pain, and maintenance of functioning through sophisticated pain-management techniques and substances; open family visitation, and a policy of no-resuscitation. The needs of the dying for pain control, social interaction, and communication with family and friends are best met either at home with medical help or in a hospice. The hospice program also supports and provides the family and patient wtih home-care services.

The hospice movement may well reflect the most important health-care philosophy to be developed in the next decade. The National Cancer Institute estimates that of every six people who get cancer, two will be saved and four will die. There is a need to provide human and cost-efficient ways of dying as medicine increases its technological skill and its ability to prolong death. The hospice movement will serve those people who have received the maximum definitive treatment, to whom no further therapy is being given, and for whom there remains an unfavorable prognosis.

THE FUNERAL INDUSTRY

The funeral director is a professional who sells the goods and services connected with the disposition of dead bodies. In some states the funeral director must be licensed and is the only one who can transport bodies and file death certificates. In other states the laws allow more freedom, but whatever the law, in the vast majority of deaths, the funeral industry will be involved in some capacity between the time of death and the final disposal of the body. At the present time, the majority of funerals involve the display of an embalmed corpse and ground burial, but the other options are:

1. Direct disposal of body from place of death to crematory with ashes buried or stored.
2. Burial or cremation with a memorial service.
3. Direct disposal of body from place of death to medical institution to be used for teaching and research.
4. Direct disposal of body to a mausoleum vault.
5. Funeral services with body cremated or entombed in mausoleum.
6. Burial at sea.

The costs of a funeral are determined by the range of services that are used. When a family uses the funeral establishment for religious or humanistic services, the cost of the funeral director's fixed operating expenses (the overhead of the physical establishment) plus a fee for the funeral director's professional services including embalming are the major costs of the average funeral. To this is added the cost of the casket and the charges for funeral vehicles. In a state where there is unit pricing of funerals (no item-by-item listing of charges), these costs represent the most common expenses of the funeral, which total $1,400 as an average price in large metropolitan areas but less in rural areas. This does not include a vault or grave site. Burial and memorial societies that individuals may join while alive or families may contract for when needed provide embalming if desired, an inexpensive casket, and minimal professional services for an average cost of $600 to $800. Direct disposal to the crematory averages $300, and body donation to a medical school may cost as much as $175 in transportation and arrangement charges. The cost of an urn for the cremated remains can be significantly less than the price of a casket and vault, further lowering the cost of some funerals. All prices are based on averages in the funeral industry.

It is clear that there is a bewildering array of alternatives from which to choose when someone dies. How is it possible to sort out all these decisions at a time when grief clouds our thinking? The answer is so simple as to be commonly overlooked. Death is an inevitable part of life, though we may wish to deny the fact. We must prepare ourselves for inescapable death by discussing our funeral choices well in advance of actual need. Funeral directors and memorial societies are pleased to discuss financial and personal arrangements at a time when we can be objective and cool-headed. Many people buy their grave sites in advance—why not plan the funeral as well? Shopping around for a funeral director makes a lot of sense if we understand that services with exactly the same casket can vary by several hundred dollars depending upon the funeral establishment used. There is no standardization in the industry. It is also possible to leave written instructions with a funeral director without actually purchasing the funeral, and in some states the law allows the prepayment of a funeral with casket selection and the deposit of funds in a bank savings account with the funeral director as a trustee to be paid upon the death of the owner of the account. These monies always belong to the depositor, and the funeral trust account can be revoked by the depositor at any time and the monies returned.

A reputable funeral director is able to be realistic about the family's financial structure and will *never* encourage a family to go into debt for a funeral. Although funeral directors may merchandise their caskets so as to highlight the desirability of the more expensive ones, the ethical funeral director will steer the family to affordable caskets without playing on their emotions. Many funeral directors are in a position to offer minimum or no-cost funerals to families in the community who are truly indigent. The funeral director is often able to collect a minimum of funds from social security death benefits ($255) and veterans' death benefits ($450), if applicable. Some funeral directors also conduct infant funerals at little or no cost. The law protects the funeral director by giving him or her the first lien for services against the estate of the deceased.

What can the funeral director do?

1. Pick up the body.
2. Arrange the funeral—time, financial arrangements.
3. Embalm the body (not required by law).
4. Provide a casket selection, provide funeral clothes if requested (extra cost).
5. Arrange for visitation (viewing) of the body by family and public.
6. Order flowers (extra cost).
7. Place death notices in local papers (extra cost).
8. Arrange for clergy to conduct services (may be extra cost in the form of an honorarium).
9. Arrange for music (usually extra cost).
10. Transport body and family to cemetery, crematory, or mausoleum.

11. Provide a vault selection for casket if required by cemetery (extra cost).
12. Arrange for grave site to be dug (extra cost).
13. Arrange for purchase of grave if necessary (extra cost).
14. Conduct grave-side services.
15. Collect death benefits and secure death certificates (extra cost).

What the funeral director cannot do:

1. Provide professional psychological services.
2. Establish the cause of death.
3. Bury or dispose of the body without written permission of the next of kin.
4. Withhold the body from the medical examiner or coroner for autopsy purposes.
5. Refuse to give up the body to another funeral director when requested by next of kin (although entitled to fair recompense for services).
6. Charge for or render services not specifically contracted for.
7. Treat the body in an undignified fashion.
8. Behave in an unethical fashion so as to influence the purchaser of funeral services to buy more expensive goods and services than the purchaser seems to be able to afford or need.

Funeral directors are usually affiliated with religious and civic organizations, so that the community can get to know them as service professionals before their services are actually needed. Most are graduates of recognized schools of mortuary science and have a minimum of two years of college. Frequently, funeral establishments are family-run businesses spanning three or four generations. A well-established firm usually advertises its long service to the community. Funeral establishments sometimes sponsor educational services for the community such as Widow to Widow programs or death education for the public schools.

The funeral director's "product" is the embalmed body. The prepared body is the focus of attention for the funeral profession. Without the body, the funeral director has little to offer in the way of goods or services. Therefore, wishes of the family that the body be quickly disposed of may be countered by arguments for "a memory picture" or "the necessity of grieving with the body present." Certainly, the dead are not able "to put their best face forward" at this time, but the funeral director's training is focused on providing as "lifelike" a corpse as possible. The family, of course, should be allowed to see the deceased as much as they wish, but we believe the finality of death should be evident in the corpse. Seeing the body is an important part of resolving the grief process, for it gives visual confirmation to the message, "This person is dead." But there is no need to wait until an embalmer "restores" the corpse before we see the body. Probably it is best to be with the dying person as death approaches or to see the body as near as possible to the time of death before it is taken to the funeral home. If we do this, it becomes easier to accept the reality of the death that is made more difficult when makeup has created the illusion of sleep or life.

Such thoughts raise value questions that are likely to come between us and the funeral director when we do business. We can be informed consumers only when we have thought through in advance what we want for ourselves and those we love. Then our interactions with the funeral industry can be clear, concise, and decisive, and we will not have to wonder whether we are making the right choices at a difficult time in our lives. The funeral director can then offer the very best professional service and fulfill the family's wishes, knowing that these services are helping the family through a significant emotional experience in a dignified, comforting way.

Life and death seemed simpler before, but now we live and die in a highly organized and all-too-often impersonal world. Teaching ourselves to be informed consumers allows us to make that complex world fit our needs and values. When we learn to make that world do what serves us best, we regain control of our living and dying. With this information, we can teach our children that an acceptance of the reality of death is really an acceptance of life.

FURTHER READING

ANNAS, GEORGE, *The Rights of Hospital Patients: The Basic ACLU Guide to a Hospital Patient's Rights.* New York: Avon Books, 1975.

ARVIO, RAYMOND, *The Cost of Dying and What You Can Do About It.* New York: Harper & Row, 1974.

DEMPSEY, DAVID, *The Way We Die: An Investigation of Death and Dying in America Today.* New York: Macmillan, 1975.

DRAZNIN, YAFFA, *How to Prepare for Death.* New York: Hawthorn, 1977.

The Editors of *Consumer Report, Funerals: Consumers' Last Rights.* New York: Norton, 1978.

ILLICH, IVAN, *Medical Nemesis: The Expropriation of Health.* New York: Bantam Books, 1977.

MORGAN, ERNEST, *A Manual of Death Education and Simple Burial.* Burnsville, N.C.: Celo Press, 1977.

Death is not a new subject in the classroom, because each culture transmits its prevailing understanding of death to its youth. Puritan children, when they learned to read from sayings about the shortness of life, also learned something about the meaning of death, as did the American Indian children when they were taught about the journey of the soul. For most of this century, Americans have been teaching children their cultural understanding of death by conspicuously not mentioning it in school except when absolutely necessary. The information transmitted to youth is that death is an enemy, alien to the natural experience of humans, and to be avoided

Politics
and Pedagogy

Chapter 9

whenever possible. The real heroes of our culture are those who seem to avoid death, so the tragic element of life is often misunderstood or thought morbid. A previously unspoken assumption is that anyone who thought too much about death was abnormal, for the progress of science and medical technology was moving the event of death further and further away from human experience, both as to the place where death occurs and its place in the life cycle. It is not an accident that children learned to avoid speaking about death openly, for it was what they were taught to do.

Education about death is changing, because the way American culture regards death is changing. It is impossible, of course, to know what the outcome of the social change will be, but it is clear that part of the change is that Americans are beginning to want their children to have more direct knowledge about death and dying and less troublesome emotional relationships with the reality of death. Whenever social attitudes and values change, the process is one of fits and starts, extreme action and reaction, lagging interest and intense interest. Months go by with little public mention of the subject, and then, as a result of some nationally publicized personal story about dying or extraordinary medical rescue from death, the topic is on everyone's lips. The change proceeds at different speeds in different parts of the culture. Some communities are full of enthusiastic parents who have informed themselves about death and dying and who are concerned that their children have a complete death education. In other communities, only the "village philosopher" has thought about the place of death education in schools. If introducing death into the classroom reflects social change, clearly the process of introducing death education will occur in fits and starts, subject to the same community differences and responding to the same vested interests as any change in the community at large.

We are concerned with how death fits into the total curriculum, for it has been largely absent. The distance between the total absence of death education in school and the total integration of it in all relevant parts of the curriculum is considerable, forcing us to look at the practical matter of how to introduce death education into schools when there is no comprehensive curriculum plan for it.

CREATING THE PERFECT EDUCATION

If we could create the perfect program for death education, how would it fit into the curriculum? Death would be part of many subject areas. In science, children would learn where life comes from and how it comes to an end. Students would know that humans are part of the nitrogen cycle, know the definitions of death and the medical and legal problems with these definitions. Since science should never be merely facts, students would have a chance to explore the values inherent in questions of life and death and knowing they would die, begin to explore the best use of the years they will have.

In social studies, children would learn about death beliefs and rituals in their own culture and in other cultures at the same time they learned about other important stages and rituals of life (puberty, marriage, and so forth). They would consider important social policy questions that are connected with death and have a chance to clarify their own values. As part of consumer education, they would learn about options in medical and funeral services and begin to prepare for the choices they will have to make. In art, music, and literature, students would explore the great creative works of our culture as their authors have tried to express themselves about death. They would discover causes for which people have been willing to die, the implications of a limited life span, and the experiences within which people who are dying and grieving find meaning.

In this perfect death education program, there would be a constant flow between students' ideas and the emotional responses they had to their world. That is, there would be a relationship between their cognitive processes and their affective processes. This means that attention would be paid to what the student knew, but at the same time, there would be an atmosphere in which the student could integrate fact with feeling.

Our way of gathering knowledge is rather fragmented in the modern world—English teachers don't teach math, and science teachers don't teach music. But in their education, perhaps toward the end of high school, students could use death as one of the foci with which to unify their life philosophies. They could find that in studying about death, the subjects of science, ethics, literature, psychology, and sociology come together at both the macrocosmic and microcosmic levels.

THE WAY IT IS

Our ideas, however, are a long way from the reality we now find in the schools. In the first place, almost nothing in death education has been done with any group of students on a comprehensive or chronological basis. Certainly no teacher in the advanced grades can plan a lesson assuming that the class will have had elementary level learning about death in an earlier grade. When an individual teacher wishes to introduce death education, it is evident that the whole content cannot be covered. The junior high school teacher in social studies or English cannot ensure that students understand in depth all the scientific questions involved. The teacher in the primary grades who does a section on knowing and feeling about death at the cognitive level of the five-to-seven-year-old cannot be sure that what has been started will be followed up later when the children are ready for more abstract learning.

It seems that for the next several years, teachers who wish to be involved with death education must accept the situation as it is, teaching with the knowledge that they are giving the students the best they can under the circumstances. As individual teachers, we cannot be responsible for the work of the entire school system. Since we assume most teachers will be working in a school system that has no set curriculum in death education, teachers must select their own goals, following their own interests as well as what they understand to be the needs of the students. The chapter on curriculum is arranged to accomplish specific goals the teacher has chosen according to the students' grade level. Thus the teacher can select specific objectives and choose from among the activities and resources suggested. There is not a great deal of material that can be brought directly into the classroom (and some that is available is not good), so death education will continue to call for the teacher's most creative work.

Although in the ideal, the various elements of death education would fit into a coherent pattern, in this book each goal and grade level is understood as a complete unit needing no past knowledge on the part of the students and demanding no follow-up teaching in the later grades. The chapter on curriculum is also designed for the ideal education, for if every teacher at each grade level carried out the suggested goals, the entire curriculum presented would be a unified whole, comprising a complete program in death education.

RESISTANCE TO DEATH EDUCATION

Some teachers, having decided to introduce death education on their own initiative, may find that there is resistance to what they are doing. So far, there have been no groups marching on local boards of education demanding that death, like sex, should only be discussed in the privacy of the home. Perhaps it would be the beginning of an interesting discussion in the community if a picket in front of school carried a sign reading, "Don't Let Them Corrupt Our Children with Death," but it probably will not happen that way. The resistance to death education is based on the fear of death and the desire to avoid thinking about it. Unlike the resistance to sex education, resistance to death education does not have organized groups. Rather, death education is likely to be met with individual noncooperation, delay, or expressions of disgust. Perhaps our experience as researchers will be of some interest to teachers. We wanted to videotape interviews with dying people. Several physicians agreed to refer patients to us "when the right one comes along." The right one never came along. The physicians saw themselves as cooperating with us, but unconsciously they could not admit that their patients were indeed dying, so we got expressions of wanting to help and no real help. Other teachers have had the same kind of frustration. One sent home permission slips for a trip to a funeral home. All came back but three. Reminders and second slips brought one of the slips. A phone call to the remaining mothers got the response, "Oh, yes, I have it somewhere and have been meaning to send it. I'll do it tomorrow morning." Only one of the slips came in, though the nonresponding mother had been prompt with money for pictures and books and other permission slips. On another student visit to a funeral home, some parents refused permission for their teenage children to go because they would get "too upset." When we discussed the possible reasons for the refusal with the parents, we were able to elicit from them that it was their own fears of dying that made them refuse permission, and we asked them to go along with us. Several teachers have reported that when a few colleagues heard they were teaching about death, they turned up their noses, saying, "What are you trying to do—frighten the children?" Their response shows who are the frightened ones.

Although the resistance to death education is not strong, it is persistent; people who want to avoid the topic find that they can do so for a long time. Perhaps the resistance is not evident because death education is not yet pervasive in school systems. Teachers can make life much easier if when they introduce the topic of death in their classrooms, they assertively but gently address themselves to parents' and colleagues' fears before those fears have a chance to turn into resistance. A good idea is to send home a note like this one which was designed for a sixth-grade class:

Dear Parents:

For the next few weeks, we will be studying many things about death and the process of dying. We will be learning the definitions of death used in medicine and in law, and the kind of decisions patients, families, and physicians sometimes have to make as people are dying. We will also be learning about social customs connected with death. We will visit a funeral home. We will compare the funeral customs of the families in the class, so students will be interviewing their parents and if possible, their grandparents. We will also study the ways people respond to death—the grief process. The children will be asking you for poems, articles, or thoughts and prayers that you have found helpful as you have faced the crisis of death or had someone you loved die.

The death of a significant person can be a very difficult experience. Even though the death was long ago, some people remain troubled. I would like to hear from you if there is anything that would be helpful for me to know about your child, or about circumstances in your family that may cause your child discomfort in studying about death. I will, of course, keep whatever you share strictly private.

Death can be a terrible thing, but with the appropriate information and a knowledge of what is happening to those around us, death is somewhat easier to face. If we keep in communication with each other about your child, together we can help your child to learn about death and dying in as free and healthy a way as possible.

Sincerely,

When parents know exactly what is to be covered, they are less fearful than when their imaginations work overtime or when they rely on the selective reports of their children. Even though the teacher asks the parents only to talk about potential problems the child might have, it is not unusual for parents to project their own anxieties onto the child. Thus, in this letter, the teacher circumvented potential resistance by allowing parents to focus anxiety onto the child, making it open, even though perhaps the parents' fears were not directly exposed.

Sometimes a person who is phobic about death or who has had a traumatic experience related to death or dying is in an administrative position in the school system. One principal, not recognizing that she was still being influenced by her fantasy surrounding her grandmother's death, insisted that it was not the place of the school to teach about death, because it raised too many anxieties in the children. Since the teacher had already started the unit, there was nothing to do but cut it short. The teacher realized too late that he had gotten some "funny looks" from the principal when he first mentioned the idea.

In general, the solution to overcoming official resistance when an individual teacher begins teaching about death seems to be to inform the parents and administration fully ahead of time, talking positively about the goals the lesson plan is to achieve and trying to get parents and administration on the teacher's side "for the good of the students." If they can't be on the teacher's side, then the next best thing is to isolate the dissenters by getting as many people to support the project as possible and thereby neutralizing the opposition. If it is very powerful opposition that cannot be neutralized, we may have to give up or be prepared to escalate the conflict to an open meeting with all the parents or the board of education. Yet lest this talk of resistance be overwhelming to some teachers, we really should add that of the scores of teachers we know who have introduced death education into their classrooms, those for whom administrative resistance was a major problem of any sort could be counted on one hand, and only one or two instances could be termed conflictive situations.

FUNERAL INDUSTRY
HELP

If there is some resistance when the individual teacher begins teaching about death, there is also some encouragement and help that must be examined carefully before use. The funeral industry in many states has welcomed death education by setting up resource kits for teachers. These are usually available at little or no cost. An increasing number of teachers who go to the local funeral director for a little help find that the funeral director is primed to help a lot more than is expected. Some of the materials the funeral industry provides are valuable basic resources helpful to the teacher. Unfortunately for the teacher, some of the publications the funeral industry has prepared are often designed to educate the public about the necessity of the funeral industry's services. The funeral industry is service oriented, but it is a profitable business. The overhead is high and the volume is low, so a good profit must be made on each funeral. If, for example, a majority of people stopped the embalming and viewing of the body, the funeral directors would not only lose the few hundred dollars they charge to embalm and make up a corpse; they would also lose the money from renting the chapel, for the body could not be kept on view for more than twenty-four hours. This, of course, would influence the selection of the casket, for the casket is bought to reflect family prestige when it is seen in the funeral home. No family visitation, no public viewing of the body, or a desire for cremation can result in the choice of a less expensive casket, which for cremation purposes, need be little more than a container. We should not be surprised, therefore, that the funeral directors' associations are trying to influence us in the educational resources they make available, showing that it is better to grieve "with the body present" or discussing the resolution of the grief process by a "memory picture" of a well-displayed corpse.

Funeral directors can be a good resource for death education, but teachers need to be wary of taking the easy way of preparation by relying too heavily on industry-prepared publications. After all, we do not teach nutrition by reading the sides of cereal boxes.

VALUES AND COMMUNITY

We hope entire school systems will develop policy guidelines for teaching about death throughout the system. Several practical and political problems should be considered as the curriculum is developed. Death curriculum must be consistent with the attitudes and customs of the community. Material that is too far from the center of communal norms will rightfully provoke objections from the community. This means that we need a careful assessment of values and attitudes in terms of the community's history and some prediction of its future. This assessment of community norms is set side by side with an analysis of the values that are inherent in the death curriculum planned. We might consult with local clergy to see if the way death is handled is at variance with the explicit and implicit values within the community. Very often the consensus of the community's opinion leaders is that the present "death system" is problematic, though there will seldom be consensus on what that system should be. By assessing attitudes and norms and making sure that the values inherent in the curriculum are not at wide variance with those norms, the introduction of death education can augment community dialogue on important issues. This, of course, does not mean that death education is only to teach the status quo. For example, if the majority of deaths in the community are in practice prolonged by the use of life-support systems and if the majority of physicians do not tell their patients when they have terminal illness, the school system does not have to teach that those things are right. The curriculum must reflect a creative tension and awareness between what is and what might be.

Since so much of death education beyond the basic biological facts involves values and emotions that are usually unexamined, if death education is to be introduced throughout the school system, values clarification and emotional self-examination opportunities should be provided for all the faculty involved. We need to be especially careful that none of the faculty involved are harboring fears and anxieties that would either prevent them from doing a good job or worse—that would raise their resistance in a way that would cause them either to do a bad job or sabotage the whole program. Values clarification is a preparation for dealing with the moral, ethical, and even theological issues that come up in death education. No one is asking that all the faculty be of one mind on values, but just as we needed to make explicit the values inherent in the curriculum, so we need to make our values as teachers explicit—even if only to ourselves.

We have outlined the need for emotional self-examination in Chapter 5. If teachers are agreeable, the school system might want to offer workshops led by qualified people that would help faculty explore their past experiences with death, their present relationships to death, and their fantasies and fears. No one should be forced to participate, but many will find this the easiest way. One of the authors conducted separate workshops for the faculty and the counseling staff before the introduction of "Death and Dying" into the school's curriculum. The counselors were able to diagnose and counsel students with death-related problems more effectively, and faculty members recommended the courses enthusiastically to students who asked questions about them. Once the staff was informed and comfortable with the material covered in the course, the teacher received assistance and cooperation from every direction. Sometimes professional in-service workshops such as those we are suggesting provide the impetus for including death education in the curriculum, because the teachers discover that they can teach about death and dying and that they are not as uncomfortable with the subject as they thought they would be.

Most faculty will need to do more than clarify their values and examine themselves, for most faculty members will find that although they are willing to teach about death, they really know very little; for they have been taught next to nothing about it. Almost every adult in the community needs remedial death education, and those who are getting ready to teach it need it most. If the school system decides to introduce death education, it will have to provide education for its faculty first. The topics to be covered are the same as those the children will cover—facts, emotional responses, consumer information, socioethical issues. Some school systems will choose to give in-service education, whereas others will choose to send their teachers to local colleges for courses.

Since many parents will be anxious about what the children are learning—a situation likely to lead to resistance—a community education program in death and dying can be instituted as a way of laying a foundation for teaching the children.

ISSUES BETWEEN HOME AND SCHOOL

1. Why should parents want children to learn about death and dying in school?

Because the school can be more objective and information centered about the subject. The kinds of resources that are available to the teacher are not available at home. The child who is presented with the facts and different ways of looking at a particular life problem has more flexibility with which to solve the problem.

2. Death is a very personal and often depressing subject, and parents may fear an outside influence on the child's emotional development.

Because this is a valid expression of parental concern, it is all the more necessary that parents take an active interest in the death education curriculum, so that optimum learning for the child can take place in an open-ended dialogue between home and school. The school is not trying to usurp parental responsibility (an argument often used against sex education) but is trying to be responsive to the needs of children whether the home recognizes the need or not. As adults, we have given up the notion that ignorance is bliss. If we try to promote this notion for our children and try to insulate them from reality, we only make them more vulnerable and less able to cope with that reality.

3. Some families, with traumatic deaths and uncomfortable memories, are worried that death education will raise feelings that they would rather suppress.

There are two ways of looking at this very real and common concern. First, if death is a painful subject for the family to discuss, then the school can present it to the child in a nonpainful way, so that the child need not be locked into the family pattern in coping with death and grief. Second, this may be viewed as an opportunity to get rid of painful and distressing feelings that may encumber the family's communications. Professional help may be indicated, whether it be counseling, therapy, or talking to a trusted advisor, but being aware of the need for help is perhaps the first and most important step to getting over a problem. With death education, maybe the child can teach us something we didn't know about death and dying, so that we can become more comfortable.

4. Some parents might wish to initiate death education where there is none.

Community support in an organized fashion is probably the most effective means of initiating a death curriculum.

Begin with the local board of education meetings or PTA groups. This book might be useful in introducing the idea to people who haven't thought of death education before. It might also be helpful to identify and speak to those teachers who would be interested in teaching it.

5. Some people do not share the religious or philosophic beliefs of the community in which they live. They are concerned with how their child will be affected by what the school teaches about death.

What we have suggested as a death curriculum in this book should not present a problem to any philosophic or religious stance, for we have tried to be as open-ended as possible in the discussion of different customs and standards. If parents think the school will reflect community values to the denigration of theirs, they should by all means speak to the teacher about their concern, so that he or she can be sensitive to the child's feelings. Perhaps parents should make a special effort to talk over classroom work with the child, so that their beliefs and principles can be reinforced as study progresses. If the family does not share the community's values, the child already knows this from interaction with school friends, so death education should not turn out to be the issue that sets the child apart in the classroom.

6. Will a death education curriculum cost more than any other similar enrichment program?

It shouldn't. Most of the materials are readily available to the teacher through normal educational sources— libraries, film centers, and so forth. There may be an initial modest outlay for teaching aids or training, but it should be no more than is normally allocated for the successful teaching of any subject. Death education can often be woven easily into existing curricula at little or no cost.

FURTHER READING

BENNETT, ROGER, "Death and the Curriculum," April 1974, Memphis State University, Memphis, Tenn. (ERIC Document Reproduction Service No. ED 093 782).

GREEN, BETTY, and DONALD IRISH, *Death Education: Preparation for Living.* Cambridge, Mass.: Schenkman Publishing Co., 1971.

LEVITON, DANIEL, and EILEEN C. FORMAN, "Death Education for Children and Youth," *Journal of Clinical Child Psychology*, 3, No. 2 (Summer 1974), 8–10.

MARTIN, JOHN HENRY, and CHARLES HARRISON, *Free To Learn: Unlocking and Ungrading American Education.* Englewood Cliffs, N.J.: Prentice-Hall, 1972.

NEWMARK, GERALD, *This School Belongs to You and Me.* New York: Hart Publishing Co., 1976.

Afterlife. An existence after death.

Anticipatory grief. Process of mourning begun before the death of a person actually occurs.

Ashes. The remains of a dead human body after cremation.

Autopsy. Examination of dead body to determine the cause of death.

Bereaved. A person suffering from the death of another.

Biopsy. The removal and examination of tissues, cells, or fluids from a living body as an aid to medical diagnosis.

Glossary

Brain death. (See appendix under Harvard Criteria for Brain Death.)

Burial permit. Necessary document secured by funeral director before final disposition of body can be made.

Cardiac arrest. Heart stoppage.

Casket. Modern term for coffin.

Cemetery. A burial ground.

Coffin. A box for burying a corpse.

Columbarium. A building or room for storage of cremation urns.

Committal. The grave-side service including burial.

Coroner. A public officer whose function is to investigate by inquest any death suspected to have resulted from other than natural causes.

Corpse. A dead body.

Cremains. The ashes of a cremated body.

Cremation. The process of reducing a dead body to ashes by burning.

Crepe. Fabric worn or draped on a doorway as a sign of mourning.

Crypt. A chamber (often underground) used as a burial place.

Death benefit. Money payable to the beneficiary of the deceased.

Death certificate. Official record of a death filed with local government.

Death wish. The conscious or unconscious desire for death of oneself or someone else.

Deceased (noun). Dead person.

Decomposition. The process of bodily decay.

Defibrillation. Restoring rhythm to a heart.

Disinter. To take out of the grave.

Electrocardiogram (EKG). The recording of changes of electrical potential taking place during the heartbeat used in diagnosing abnormalities.

Electroencephalogram (EEG). The recording of brain waves.

Embalm. To treat a dead body so as to sanitize it for viewing purposes.

Entombment. Burial in a mausoleum (see *mausoleum*).

Estate. The assets and liabilities left by a person at death.

Eulogy. A speech of high praise (especially for the dead).

Euthanasia (passive and active). Literally: the good death. Generally interpreted as release from suffering. Passive: No medical intervention in the process of dying; this is often acceptable medical practice. Active: Intervention that hastens an inevitable death; not acceptable medical practice.

Execu(tor/trix). A person appointed to carry out a will.

Funeral director. One who manages funerals and is usually a licensed embalmer.

Funeral home. An establishment with facilities for preparing the dead for cremation or burial, for viewing bodies, and for funerals.

Funeral service. Observances held for the dead before burial or cremation.

Grave. An excavation for burial of a body.

Graveyard. See *cemetery*.

Grief. A deep poignant distress caused by bereavement.

Headstone. See *monument.*

Hearse. A vehicle for conveying the dead to the grave.

Heaven. A place for the blessed dead to exist in communication with God. (Religious interpretation)

Hell. A place in which the damned suffer everlasting punishment. (Religious interpretation)

Heroic measures. Medical machinery and practices used to delay death, such as respirators for breathing and heart massage for stopped hearts.

Immortality. Exemption from death.

Interment. Burying of the dead.

Intestate. Having left no will.

Kaddish. A Jewish prayer recited after the death of a friend or relative.

Last rites. Religious rituals for the purpose of easing the transition from life to death.

Living Will. See appendix.

Mass. A celebration of the Eucharist especially in accordance with Catholic rites.

Mausoleum. A building for above-ground burial of bodies.

Medical examiner. A public official, usually a physician, whose function is to ascertain the causes and circumstances of violent or criminal deaths.

Memorial service. Ceremony conducted without the body present or after the burial.

Monument. A stone erected in remembrance of the dead.

Mortician. See *funeral director.*

Mortuary. A place where dead bodies are kept until burial (see also *funeral home*).

Mourner. See *bereaved.*

Mourning. The act of sorrowing; an outward sign of grief for a person's death; a period of time at which signs of grief are shown.

Necrophilia. Obsession with and usually erotic interest in corpses.

Nitrogen cycle. A continuous series of natural processes by which nitrogen passes through successive stations in air, soil, and organisms; a cycle of growth, death, decay, and reuse by new organisms.

Obituary. A notice of a person's death, usually with a short biographical account.

Organ transplant. To transfer an organ or tissue from one individual to another.

Pall. A heavy cloth draped over a coffin.

Pallbearer. A person who helps carry a coffin at a funeral.

Plot. A small piece of land in a cemetery.

Postdeath contact. Experiences of interaction between the living and the dead in some sensory mode (hearing, seeing, feeling) usually shortly after the death occurs.

Postmortem. See *autopsy.*

Putrefaction. The decomposition of organic matter.

Reincarnation. A rebirth (usually of a soul) in a new body or form of life. (Religious interpretation)

Remains. A dead human body.

Restoration. To make the dead body look as "lifelike" as possible for viewing purposes.

Resurrection. To rise from the dead.

Resuscitation. The revival from apparent death or unconsciousness.

Shiva. Seven-day period of formal mourning following the funeral of a close relative (Judaism).

Shroud. A cloth or ritual garments used to wrap a body for burial.

Soul. Nonmaterial spiritual essence of an individual life.

Thanatology. The study of death and dying.

Thanatos. The instinctual desire for death (Greek).

Undertaker. See *funeral director*. Originally applied to the person who "undertook" the necessary tasks for burial of the dead.

Urn. A container used for holding ashes of the dead.

Vault. A grave liner generally made of concrete or other rigid material to hold the coffin.

Viewing (visitation). Physical display of the deceased in the funeral chapel.

Wake. Watch over the body of a dead person prior to the funeral (Christian) or the ritual of visitation preceding the funeral.

Widow/widower. A woman or man who has lost a spouse by death and has not remarried.

Will. A legal declaration as to the disposition of one's estate after death.

1. HARVARD CRITERIA FOR BRAIN DEATH

A Definition of Irreversible Coma

CHARACTERISTICS OF IRREVERSIBLE COMA

An organ, brain or other, that no longer functions and has no possibility of functioning again is for all practical purposes dead. Our first problem is to determine the characteristics of a permanently nonfunctioning brain.

A patient in this state appears to be in deep coma. The condition can be satisfactorily diagnosed by points 1, 2,

Appendix

and 3 to follow. The electroencephalogram (point 4) provides confirmatory data, and when available it should be utilized. In situations where for one reason or another electroencephalographic monitoring is not available, the absence of cerebral function has to be determined by purely clinical signs, to be described, or by absence of circulation as judged by standstill of blood in the retinal vessels, or by absence of cardiac activity.

1. Unreceptivity and Unresponsibility. There is a total unawareness to externally applied stimuli and inner need and complete unresponsiveness—our definition of irreversible coma. Even the most intensely painful stimuli evoke no vocal or other response, not even a groan, withdrawal of a limb, or quickening of respiration.

2. No Movements or Breathing. Observations covering a period of at least one hour by physicians are adequate to satisfy the criteria of no spontaneous muscular movements or spontaneous respiration or response to stimuli such as pain, touch, sound, or light. After the patient is on a mechanical respirator, the total absence of spontaneous breathing may be established by turning off the respirator for three minutes and observing whether there is any effort on the part of the subject to breathe spontaneously. (The respirator may be turned off for this time provided that at the start of the trial period the patient's carbon dioxide tension is within the normal range, and provided also that the patient had been breathing room air for at least 10 minutes prior to the trial.)

3. No reflexes. Irreversible coma with abolition of

Reprinted from the JOURNAL OF THE AMERICAN MEDICAL ASSOCIATION, August 5, 1968, Vol. 205, pp. 337–340. Copyright 1968 by American Medical Association.

central nervous system activity is evidenced in part by the absence of elicitable reflexes. The pupil will be fixed and dilated and will not respond to a direct source of bright light. Since the establishment of a fixed, dilated pupil is clear-cut in clinical practice there should be no uncertainty as to its presence. Ocular movement (to head turning and to irrigation of the ears with ice water) and blinking are absent. There is no evidence of postural activity (decerebrate or other). Swallowing, yawning, vocalization are in abeyance. Corneal and pharyngeal reflexes are absent.

As a rule the stretch of tendon reflexes cannot be elicited; i.e., tapping the tendons of the biceps, triceps, and pronator muscles, quadriceps and gastrocnemius muscles with the reflex hammer elicits no contraction of the respective muscles. Plantar or noxious stimulation gives no response.

4. Flat Electroencephalogram. Of great confirmatory value is the flat or isoelectric EEG. We must assume that the electrodes have been properly applied, that the apparatus is functioning normally and that the personnel in charge is competent. We consider it prudent to have one channel of the apparatus used for an electrocardiogram. This channel will monitor the ECG so that, if it appears in the electroencephalographic leads because of high resistance, it can be readily identified. It also establishes the presence of the active heart in the absence of the EEG. We recommend that another channel be used for a noncephalic lead. This will pick up space-borne or vibration-borne artifacts and identify them. The simplest form of such a monitoring noncephalic electrode has two leads over the dorsum of the hand, preferably the right hand, so the ECG will be minimal or absent. Since one of the requirements of this state is that there be no muscle activity,

these two dorsal hand electrodes will not be bothered by muscle artifact. The apparatus should be run at standard gains 10 μv/mm, 50 μv/5 mm. Also it should be isoelectric at double this standard gain which is 5 μv/mm or 25 μv/5 mm. At least ten full minutes of recording are desirable, but twice that would be better.

It is also suggested that the gains at some point be opened to their full amplitude for a brief period (5 to 100 seconds) to see what is going on. Usually in an intensive care unit artifacts will dominate the picture, but these are readily identifiable. There shall be no electroencephalographic response to noise or to pinch.

All of the above tests shall be repeated at least 24 hours later with no change.

The validity of such data as indications of irreversible cerebral damage depends on the exclusion of two conditions: hypothermia (temperature between 90°F (32.2°C) or central nervous system depressants, such as barbiturates.

2. A LIVING WILL

To any medical facility in whose care i happen to be
To any individual who may become responsible for my
health, welfare or affairs

Death is as much a reality as birth, growth, maturity and old age—it is the one certainty of life. If the time comes when I, _____, can no longer take part in decisions for my own future, let this statement stand as an expression of my wishes, while I am still of sound mind.

If the situation should arise in which there is no reasonable expectation of my recovery from physical or mental disability, I request that I be allowed to die and not be kept alive by artificial means or "heroic measures." I do not fear death itself as much as the indignities of deterioration, dependence and hopeless pain. I, therefore, ask that medication be mercifully administered to me to alleviate suffering even though this may hasten the moment of death.

This request is made after careful consideration. I hope you who care for me will feel morally bound to follow its mandate. I recognize that this appears to place a heavy responsibility upon you, but it is with the intention of relieving you of such responsibility and of placing it upon myself in accordance with my strong convictions, that this statement is made.

Reprinted with the permission of the Concern for Dying, 250 West 57th Street, New York, New York 10019. Copies are available upon request.

Signed   _____

Date   _____

Witness   _____

Witness   _____

Copies of this request have been given to   _____

_____

_____

_____

3. UNIFORM
ANATOMICAL
GIFT ACT

(Copy of final draft as approved on July 30, 1968, by the National Conference of Commissioners on Uniform State Laws.)
An act authorizing the gift of all or part of a human body after death for specified purposes.

SECTION 1. (Definitions)

(a) "Bank or storage facility" means a facility licensed, accredited or approved under the laws of any state for storage of human bodies or parts thereof.

Reprinted with the permission of the American Medical Association from the JOURNAL OF THE AMERICAN MEDICAL ASSOCIATION, Vol. 206, p. 2501 ff., December 9, 1968.

(b) "Decedent" means a deceased individual and includes a stillborn infant or fetus.

(c) "Donor" means an individual who makes a gift of all or part of his body.

(d) "Hospital" means a hospital licensed, accredited or approved under the laws of any state and includes a hospital operated by the United States government, a state or a subdivision thereof, although not required to be licensed under state laws.

(e) "Part" includes organs, tissues, eyes, bones, arteries, blood, other fluids and other portions of a human body, and "part" includes "parts."

(f) "Person" means an individual, corporation, government or governmental subdivision or agency, business trust, estate, trust, partnership or association or any other legal entity.

(g) "Physician" or "surgeon" means a physician or surgeon licensed or authorized to practice under the laws of any state.

(h) "State" includes any state, district, commonwealth, territory, insular possession, and any other area subject to the legislative authority of the United States of America.

SECTION 2. (Persons Who May Execute an Anatomical Gift)

(a) Any individual of sound mind and 18 years of age or more may give all or any part of his body for any purposes specified in section 3, the gift to take effect upon death.

(b) Any of the following persons, in order of priority stated, when persons in prior classes are not available at the time of death, and in the absence of actual notice of contrary indications by the decedent, or actual notice of opposition by a member of the same or a prior class, may give all or any part of the decedent's body for any purposes specified in section 3.

(1) the spouse,

(2) an adult son or daughter,

(3) either parent,

(4) an adult brother or sister,

(5) a guardian of the person of the decedent at the time of his death,

(6) any other person authorized or under obligation to dispose of the body.

(c) If the donee has actual notice of contrary indications by the decedent, or that a gift by a member of a class is opposed by a member of the same or a prior class, the donee shall not accept the gift. The persons authorized by subsection (b) may make the gift after death or immediately before death.

(d) A gift of all or part of a body authorizes any examination necessary to assure medical acceptability of the gift for the purposes intended.

(e) The rights of the donee created by the gift are paramount to the rights of others except as provided by section 7 (d).

SECTION 3. (Persons Who May Become Donees, and Purposes for Which Anatomical Gifts May Be Made) The following persons may become donees of gifts of bodies or parts thereof for the purposes stated:

(1) any hospital, surgeon, or physician, for medical or dental education, research, advancement of medical or dental science, therapy or transplantation; or

(2) any accredited medical or dental school, college or university for education, research, advancement of medical or dental science or therapy; or

(3) any bank or storage facility for medical or dental education, research, advancement of medical or dental science, therapy or transplantation; or

(4) any specified individual for therapy or transplantation needed by him.

SECTION 4. (Manner of Executing Anatomical Gifts)

(a) A gift of all or part of the body under section 2 (a) may be made by will. The gift becomes effective upon the death of the testator without waiting for probate. If the will is not probated, or if it is declared invalid for testamentary purposes, the gift, to the extent that it has been acted upon in good faith, is nevertheless valid and effective.

(b) A gift of all or part of the body under section 2 (a) may also be made by document other than a will. The gift becomes effective upon the death of the donor. The document, which may be a card designed to be carried on the person, must be signed by the donor, in the presence of 2 witnesses who must sign the document in his presence. If the donor cannot sign, the document may be signed for him at his direction and in his presence, and in the presence of 2 witnesses who must sign the document in his presence. Delivery of the document of gift during the donor's lifetime is not necessary to make the gift valid.

(c) The gift may be made to a specified donee or without specifying a donee. If the latter, the gift may be accepted by the attending physician as donee upon or following death. If the gift is made to a specified donee who is not available at the time and place of death, the attending physician upon or following death, in the absence of any expressed indication that the donor desired otherwise, may accept the gift as donee. The physician who becomes a donee under this subsection shall not participate in the procedures for removing or transplanting a part.

(d) Notwithstanding section 7 (b), the donor may designate in his will, card or other document of gift the surgeon or physician to carry out the appropriate procedures. In the absence of a designation, or if the designee is not available, the donee or other person authorized to accept the gift may employ or authorize any surgeon or physician for the purpose.

(e) Any gift by a person designated in section 2 (b) shall be made by a document signed by him, or made by his telegraphic, recorded telephonic or other recorded message.

SECTION 5. (Delivery of Document of Gift) If the gift is made by the donor to a specified donee, the will, card, or other document, or an executed copy thereof, may be delivered to the donee to expedite the appropriate procedures immediately after death, but delivery is not necessary to the validity of the gift. The will, card or other document, or an executed copy thereof, may be deposited in any hospital, bank or storage facility or registry office that accepts them for safekeeping or for facilitation of procedures after death. On request of any interested party upon or after the donor's death, the person in possession shall produce the document for examination.

SECTION 6. (Amendment or Revocation of the Gift)

(a) If the will, card or other document or executed copy thereof has been delivered to a specified donee, the donor may amend or revoke the gift by:

(1) the execution and delivery to the donee of a signed statement, or

(2) an oral statement made in the presence of 2 persons and communicated to the donee, or

(3) a statement during a terminal illness or injury addressed to an attending physician and communicated to the donee, or

(4) a signed card or document found on his person or in his effects.

(b) Any document of gift which has not been delivered to the donee may be revoked by the donor in the manner set out in subsection (a) or by destruction, cancellation, or mutilation of the document and all executed copies thereof.

(c) Any gift made by a will may also be amended or revoked in the manner provided for amendment or revocation of wills, or as provided in subsection (a).

SECTION 7. (Rights and Duties at Death)

(a) The donee may accept or reject the gift. If the donee accepts a gift of the entire body, he may, subject to the terms of the gift, authorize embalming and the use of the body in funeral services. If the gift is of a part of the body, the donee, upon the death of the donor and prior to embalming, shall cause the part to be removed without unnecessary mutilation. After removal of the part, custody of the remainder of the body vests in the surviving spouse, next of kin or other persons under obligation to dispose of the body.

(b) The time of death shall be determined by a physician who attends the donor at his death, or, if none, the physician who certifies the death. This physician shall not participate in the procedures for removing or transplanting a part.

(c) A person who acts in good faith in accord with the terms of this Act, or under the anatomical gift laws of another state (or a foreign country) is not liable for damages in any civil action or subject to prosecution in any criminal proceedings for his act.

(d) The provisions of this Act are subject to the laws of this state prescribing powers and duties with respect to autopsies.

SECTION 8. (Uniformity of Interpretation) This Act shall be so construed as to effectuate its general purpose to make uniform the law of those states which enact it.

SECTION 9. (Short Title) This Act may be cited as the Uniform Anatomical Gift Act.

4. STATUTE OF THE STATE OF KANSAS

77-202 Definition of death. A person will be considered medically and legally dead if, in the opinion of a physician, based on ordinary standards of medical practice, there is the absence of spontaneous respiratory and cardiac function and, because of the disease or condition which caused, directly or indirectly, these functions to cease, or because of the passage of time since these functions ceased, attempts at resuscitation are considered hopeless; and, in this event, death will have occurred at the time these functions ceased; or

A person will be considered medically and legally dead if, in the opinion of a physician, based on ordinary standards of medical practice, there is the absence of spontaneous brain function; and if based on ordinary standards of medical practice, during reasonable attempts to either maintain or restore spontaneous circulatory or respiratory function in the absence of aforesaid brain function, it appears that further attempts at resuscitation or supportive maintenance will not succeed, death will have occurred at the time when these conditions first coincide. Death is to be pronounced before artificial means of supporting respiratory and circulatory function are terminated and before any vital organ is removed for purposes of transplantation.

These alternative definitions of death are to be utilized for all purposes in this state, including the trials of civil and criminal cases, any laws to the contrary notwithstanding. (L. 1970, ch. 378, 1; July 1.)

5. ARKANSAS LIVING WILL LEGISLATION

Act 879 (H.B. 826) Enacted: March, 1977
Introduced by Representative Henry Wilkins III 2/24/77
Passed by House (52–3) 3/14/77
Passed by Senate (32–0) 3/17/77
Signed by Governor David Pryor 3/30/77

AN ACT to permit an individual to request or refuse in writing medical or surgical means or procedures calculated to prolong his life; and to authorize such request or refusal by others on behalf of one incompetent or under 18; and for other purposes.

BE IT ENACTED BY THE GENERAL ASSEMBLY OF THE STATE OF ARKANSAS:

SECTION 1.

Every person shall have the right to die with dignity and to refuse and deny the use or application by any person of artificial, extraordinary, extreme or radical medical or surgical means or procedures calculated to prolong his life. Alternatively, every person shall have the right to request that such extraordinary means be utilized to prolong life to the extent possible.

SECTION 2.

Any person, with the same formalities as are required by the laws of this State for the execution of a will, may execute a document exercising such right and refusing and denying the use or application by any person of artificial, extraordinary, extreme or radical medical or surgical means or procedures calculated to prolong his life. In the alternative, any person may request in writing that all means be utilized to prolong life.

SECTION 3.

If any person is a minor or an adult who is physically or mentally unable to execute or is otherwise incapacitated from executing either document, it may be executed in the same form on his behalf:

(a) By either parent of the minor;

(b) By his spouse;

(c) If his spouse is unwilling or unable to act, by his child aged eighteen or over;

(d) If he has more than one child aged eighteen or over, by a majority of such children;

(e) If he has no spouse or child aged eighteen or over, by either of his parents;

(f) If he has no parent living, by his nearest living relative; or

(g) If he is mentally incompetent, by his legally appointed guardian. Provided, that a form executed in compliance with this Section must contain a signed statement by two physicians that extraordinary means would have to be utilized to prolong life.

SECTION 4.

Any person, hospital or other medical institution which acts or refrains from acting in reliance on and in compliance with such document shall be immune from liability otherwise arising out of such failure to use or apply artificial, extraordinary, extreme or radical medical or surgical means or procedures calculated to prolong such person's life.

SECTION 5.

All laws and parts of laws in conflict with this Act are hereby repealed.

6. AMERICAN HOSPITAL ASSOCIATION PATIENT'S BILL OF RIGHTS

The American Hospital Association presents a Patient's Bill of Rights with the expectation that observance of these rights will contribute to more effective patient care and greater satisfaction for the patient, his physician, and the hospital organization. Further, the Association presents these rights in the expectation that they will be supported by the hospital on behalf of its patients, as an integral part of the healing process. It is recognized that a personal relationship between the physician and the patient is essential for the provision of proper medical care. The traditional physician–patient relationship takes on a new dimension when care is rendered within an organizational structure. Legal precedent has established that the institution itself also has a responsibility to the patient. It is in recognition of these factors that these rights are affirmed.

1. The patient has the right to considerate and respectful care.
2. The patient has the right to obtain from his physician complete current information concerning his diagnosis, treatment, and prognosis in terms the patient can be reasonably expected to understand. When it is not medically advisable to give such information to the patient, the information should be made available to an appropriate person in his behalf. He has the right to know by name, the physician responsible for coordinating his care.

(Reprinted, with permission, from *Patient's Bill of Rights*, published by the American Hospital Association.)

*3. The patient has the right to receive from his physician information necessary to give informed consent prior to the start of any procedure and/or treatment. Except in emergencies, such information for informed consent, should include but not necessarily be limited to the specific procedure and/or treatment, the medically significant risks involved, and the probable duration of incapacitation. Where medically significant alternatives for care or treatment exist, or when the patient requests information concerning medical alternatives, the patient has the right to such information. The patient also has the right to know the name of the person responsible for the procedures and/or treatment.

*4. The patient has the right to refuse treatment to the extent permitted by law, and to be informed of the medical consequences of his action.

5. The patient has the right to every consideration of his privacy concerning his own medical care program. Case discussion, consultation, examination and treatment are confidential and should be conducted discreetly. Those not directly involved in his care must have the permission of the patient to be present.

6. The patient has the right to expect that all communications and records pertaining to his care should be treated as confidential.

7. The patient has the right to expect that within its capacity a hospital must make reasonable response to the request of a patient for services. The hospital must provide evaluation, service, and/or referral as indicated by the urgency of the case. When medically permissible a patient may be transferred to another facility only after he has received complete information and explanation concerning the needs for alternatives to such a transfer. The institution to which the patient is to be transferred must first have accepted the patient for transfer.

8. The patient has the right to obtain information as to any relationship of his hospital to other health care and educational institutions insofar as his care is concerned. The patient has the right to obtain information as to the existence of any professional relationships among individuals, by name, who are treating him.

*Reprinted by Euthanasia Educational Council, 250 West 57th Street, New York, N.Y. 10019.

*9. The patient has the right to be advised if the hospital proposes to engage in or perform human experimentation affecting his care or treatment. The patient has the right to refuse to participate in such research projects.

10. The patient has the right to expect reasonable continuity of care. He has the right to know in advance what appointment times and physicians are available and where. The patient has the right to expect that the hospital will provide a mechanism whereby he is informed by his physician or a delegate of the physician of the patient's continuing health care requirements following discharge.

11. The patient has the right to examine and receive an explanation of his bill regardless of source of payment.

12. The patient has the right to know what hospital rules and regulations apply to his conduct as a patient.

No catalogue of rights can guarantee for the patient the kind of treatment he has a right to expect. A hospital has many functions to perform, including the prevention and treatment of disease, the education of both health-care professionals and patients, and the conduct of clinical research. All these activities must be conducted with an overriding concern for the patient, and, above all, the recognition of his dignity as a human being. Success in achieving this recognition assures success in the defense of the rights of the patient.

7. AMERICAN CIVIL LIBERTIES UNION MODEL PATIENT'S BILL OF RIGHTS

Preamble

As you enter this health care facility, it is our duty to remind you that your health care is a cooperative effort between you as a patient and the doctors and hospital staff. During your stay you will have a patient's rights advocate available. The duty of the advocate is to assist you in all the decisions you must make and in all situations in which your health and welfare are at stake. The advocate's first responsibility is to help you understand who each of the people are who will be working with you and to help you understand what your rights as a patient are. Your advocate can be reached at any time of the day by dialing _____ . The following is a list of your rights as a patient. Your advocate's duty is to see to it that you are afforded these rights. You should call your advocate whenever you have any questions or concerns about any of these rights.

1. The patient has a legal right to informed participation in all decisions involving his health care program.

2. We recognize the right of all potential patients to know what research and experimental protocols are being used in our facility and what alternatives are available in the community.

3. The patient has a legal right to privacy respecting the source of payment for treatment and care. This right includes access to the highest degree of care without regard to the source of payment for that treatment and care.

4. We recognize the right of a potential patient to complete and accurate information concerning medical care and procedures.

5. The patient has a legal right to prompt attention especially in an emergency situation.

6. The patient has a legal right to a clear, concise explanation of all proposed procedures in layman's terms, including the possibilities of any risk of mortality or serious side effects, problems related to recuperation, and probability of success, and will not be subjected to any procedure without his voluntary, competent, and understanding consent. The specifics of such consent shall be set out in a written consent form, signed by the patient.

7. The patient has a legal right to a clear, complete, and accurate evaluation of his condition and prognosis without treatment before he is asked to consent to any test or procedure.

8. We recognize the right of the patient to know the identity and professional status of all those providing service. All personnel have been instructed to introduce themselves, state their status, and explain their role in the health care of the patient. Part of this right is the right of the patient to know the physician responsible for his care.

9. We recognize the right of the patient who does not speak English to have access to an interpreter.

10. The patient has a legal right to all the information contained in his medical record while in the health-care facility and to examine the record upon request.

11. We recognize the right of a patient to discuss his condition with a consultant specialist at his own request and his own expense.

12. The patient has a legal right not to have any test or procedure, designed for educational purposes rather than his direct personal benefit, performed on him.

13. The patient has a legal right to refuse any particular drug, test, procedure, or treatment.

14. The patient has a legal right to both personal and informational privacy with respect to: the hospital staff, other doctors, residents, interns and medical students, researchers, nurses, other hospital personnel, and other patients.

15. We recognize the patient's right to access to people outside the health care facility by means of visitors and the telephone. Parents may stay with their children and relatives with terminally ill patients 24 hours a day.

16. The patient has a legal right to leave the health care facility regardless of physical condition or financial status, although he may be requested to sign a release stating that he is leaving against the medical judgment of his doctor or the hospital.

17. No patient may be transferred to another facility unless he has received a complete explanation of the desirability and need for the transfer, the other facility has accepted the patient for trans-

fer, and the patient has agreed to transfer. If the patient does not agree to transfer, the patient has the right to a consultant's opinion on the desirability of transfer.

18. A patient has a right to be notified of discharge at least one day before it is accomplished, to demand a consultation by an expert on the desirability of discharge, and to have a person of the patient's choice so notified.

19. The patient has a right, regardless of source of payment, to examine and receive an itemized and detailed explanation of his total bill for services rendered in the facility.

20. The patient has a right to competent counseling from the facility to help him obtain financial assistance from public or private sources to meet the expense of services received in the institution.

21. The patient has a right to timely prior notice of the termination of his eligibility for reimbursement for the expense of his care by any third-party payer.

22. At the termination of his stay at the hospital care facility we recognize the right of a patient to a complete copy of the information contained in his medical record.

23. We recognize the right of all patients to have 24 hour a day access to a patient's rights advocate who may act on behalf of the patient to assert or protect the rights set out in his document

8. COPY OF A
DEATH CERTIFICATE

Illinois Department of Public Health—Office of Vital Records (based on 1978 U.S. Standard Certificate).

9. A CRABBIT OLD WOMAN WROTE THIS

What do you see nurses, what do you see?
Are you thinking when you are looking at me—
A crabbit old woman, not very wise,
Uncertain of habit, with far away eye,
Who dribbles her food and makes no reply
When you say in a loud voice—I do wish you'd try.
Who seems not to notice the things that you do,
And forever is losing a stocking or shoe.
Who, unresisting or not, lets you do as you will,
With bathing and feeding, the long day to fill.
Is that what you are thinking? Is that what you see?
Then open your eyes, nurse, you're looking at me.
I tell you who I am as I sit here so still;
As I use at your bidding, as I eat at your will,
I'm a small child often with a father and mother,
Brothers and sisters, who love one another.
A young girl of sixteen, with wings on her feet.
Dreaming that soon now a lover she'll meet;
A bride soon a-twenty, my heart gives a leap,
Remembering the vows that I promised to keep;
At twenty-five now I have young of my own,
Who need me to build a secure, happy home;
A woman of thirty, my young now grow fast,
Bound to each other with ties that should last.
At forty, my young sons have grown and gone,
But my man's beside me to see I don't mourn.
At fifty, once more babies play round my knee,
Again we know children, my loved one and me.
Dark days are upon me, my husband is dead,
I look to the future, I shudder with dread.
For my young are all rearing young of their own,
And I think of the years and the love that I've known.
I'm now an old woman and nature is cruel—
'Tis jest to make old age look like a fool.

The body it crumbles, grace and vigour depart,
There now is a stone where I once had a heart.
But inside this old carcass a young girl still dwells,
And now again my battered heart swells.
I remember the joys, I remember the pain.
And I'm loving and living life over again.
I think of the years all too few gone too fast,
And accept the stark fact that nothing can last
So open your eyes, nurses, open and see,
NOT, a crabbit old woman, LOOK closer,

SEE ME!

—*Anonymous*

Index